INTEGRITY

... The Missing Link

DR. NOSIKE M. ERONDU

INTEGRITY... The Missing Link

ISBN: 978-978-781-884-8

Published and Printed By:

13 Etta Agbo Avenue,
Calabar, Cross River State, Nigeria 08056278313, 08023994480
E-mail: freshdewcoy@gmail.com, justinita@ymail.com

All Scripture quotations, unless otherwise indicated, are taken from the King James Version (KJV).

Dedication

This book is dedicated first and foremost to God Almighty who caused me to know Him, not just about Him. I would have ordinarily wallowed and got lost in religion or "churchianity". He has sustained me since that May 16th 1987 when I accepted Him in my life as Lord and Savour till date, despite my many and obvious weaknesses, and He is not yet tired of doing so. Only Him qualified me to write this book. Nothing else could.

I also dedicate this book to those men and women who have exhibited a life of integrity in all their worldly endeavours. My example is Mr Peter Gregory Obi-former governor of Anambra State Nigeria, and the presidential candidate of the Labour Party in 2023 general elections in Nigeria. I have never known of any politician in Nigeria like him!

Finally, I dedicate this book to my late father, Chief Sir M, E, Onukogu who was an epitome of integrity in his life time. May his soul Rest In Perfect Peace.

CONTENTS

ACKNOWLEDGEMENT

I will first and foremost acknowledge the Lord God Almighty who by the inspiration of His Holy Spirit inspired me to write this book even in my total unworthiness. Despite my procrastination and foot dragging, He was patient with me, and when I showed some signs of readiness, He enabled me to commence. Even when for personal reasons I suspended the writing midway for more than one year, He waited for me. When I was convinced to continue, He was able to restore the ability and the needed wisdom and knowledge. What could I have done without His enablement by His Spirit? To Him alone be all the glory and honor for leading me to the finishing point despite the time it has taken to do so.

I must also acknowledge my wife, my heartthrob, Mrs Constance Chidinma Erondu for all the encouragement she gave me, always asking me how the writing of the book was going. She was a great inspiration for me to continue as she has always been in all my endeavours since our marriage almost 33 years ago.

I received great help from Apostle David Onuoha and Prof Godwin I.N, Emezue for both, reading through the manuscript and meticulously making wonderful corrections and contributing great ideas to make the book what it is today.

I will not forget my bosom friend indeed, Dr Sunny Jackson, who loves me lavishly for reasons I do not know. He produced all the copies of the manuscripts needed at various times with his own materials free of charge.

To all of you, I say you will never lack help or assistance whenever you need it.

PREFACE

It has been nearly ten years since the inspiration to write this book on integrity came. I remember it first came to me as a ministration in my spirit one day some years ago when a man of God (I have honestly forgotten his name)came to minister in my chapter of the Full Gospel Business Men's Fellowship International (FGBMFI), known as Umuahia Main Chapter. The man of God ministered on INTEGRITY for about forty five minutes or so. As he was speaking, I received what I will call a nudge in my spirit that I should later write a book on this topic. It actually looked like a dream and I took it with a "pinch of salt" wondering when I will ever have the time to do that because I knew my hands were full with so many things. However, because of the ministration I received, I decided to put down a few things on a small sheet of paper, mainly headlines and a few verses of scripture as he was preaching. At the end I put the piece of paper inside my Bible. But somehow it became a burden after a while especially each time I flipped the Bible and saw that piece of paper there.

The next thing I did was that I started scribbling some

things, like scriptures on that sheet of paper, especially each time I read anything about integrity. I kept receiving the nudge to start until about six years ago when I started writing gradually whenever I had a spare time in my office. I noticed that my office was the most convenient place I could stay to write or even remember to write.

After writing the first five chapters, something happened that discouraged or disillusioned me, so I stopped. And for more than one year, I did not write again. But one day, the Spirit of God spoke to me again in a very un-peculiar way and urged me to continue. But by this time I had lost the flow and the sequence. I prayed and asked for divine enablement, and I received the ministration to go back and read all that I had already written to get back on track.

One other thing that made me very desirous of writing this book on integrity was that I found out that indeed there has been an embarrassing level of erosion of integrity in all spheres of our society, even in the church of Jesus Christ. In fact, lack of integrity is said to be the second type of AIDS that has afflicted our society. It is called Acute Integrity Deficiency Syndrome.(AIDS)

Our people are now beginning to think that integrity no longer pays, because corruption is now being celebrated. That is a lie from the pit of hell. The belief in many quarters now is that you must cut corners in order to have success in your endeavours. It has even got to an extent in our society where friends, associates, and relatives, and even colleagues begin to mock you if you insist on exhibiting integrity in your duties, business or professional practice.

Unfortunately the younger generation are beginning to believe the lie and it has led them into all forms of fraudulent activities because of the get rich quick syndrome.

The essence of this book is to reiterate the fact that God's standard has not changed (Ps 119:89), and that He still expects us to exhibit integrity in all our endeavours , and of course to show that He God still rewards integrity.

I do hope that you will learn a few things that will open your eyes to what integrity means and to imbibe that spirit and advertise it. Happy reading.

FOREWORD

Reading through the manuscript of the book titled "INTEGRITY, *THE MISSING LINK*" is like listening to the prototypical Dr Nosike Erondu-National Director of the Full Gospel Business Mens's Fellowship International-Nigeria, Umuahia Zone-preaching or teaching the word of God. The customary passion is there, the conviction is there, and the courage to present the subject of integrity as he perceives it is there.

The author succinctly defines and explains his understanding of the concept of integrity and laments the dearth of integrity in the churches, institutions, organisations and other places in Nigeria where integrity is expected to be treated as sacrosanct. He is as unsparing in the condemnation of the dearth of integrity as he is lavish in his praise of the few instances where integrity has been exhibited by some individuals

I feel superbly elated that Dr Erondu considered me worthy to appraise the manuscript and do a critique of it. In asking me also to write a foreword, I am most grateful.

I can boldly say that this book is a product of a man who craves integrity, breathes integrity, eats integrity and drinks integrity. It is written in the lucid and conversational language of a Bible teacher and the aggressiveness of a soul hunter. In this book, Dr Erondu exhibits a boldness that seems to challenge the reader to fault the writer if possible. It's like the writer is saying "fault me if you can. What I have written about the desirability of integrity is what I practice."

Generally, I have a feeling that this book is a product of Dr Erondu's understanding of Proverbs 10 vs 9: *"Whoever walks in integrity, walks securely, but whoever takes crooked paths will be found out"* (NIV).

It is therefore, my prayer that all who will read this book shall commend the author for taking a bold step, to canvass in these pages, for the restoration of integrity in our society.

Professor Godwin I. N Emezue
Field Representative
(FGBMFI-Nigeria)
Deputy Vice –Chancellor (Academic)
Abia State University, Uturu.

INTRODUCTION

A couple of times in the recent past, some commercial (taxi) drivers had been celebrated in our nation (Nigeria) for returning items that their passengers forgot in their vehicles. Most of the times these items are huge sums of money in different currencies. At other times somebody overpaid with a huge amount of money by the bank returns it and was also celebrated. A few of those people end up receiving national honours from the president. Others are handsomely rewarded by the owners of the items returned.

You may ask; why should we make such noise that some people returned what do not belong to them?

People have also received accolades, honors, prizes, promotions and appointments either for distinguishing themselves in service, or for bringing development to their people, for making judicious use of public funds entrusted to them. Some have fought gallantly as security officers (police, army, Navy, Airforce etc) in defence of their fatherland even to the point of losing their lives or being terribly wounded and deformed permanently. These people have also been elaborately honoured, sometimes post humously.

You may also ask why all this funfare for some persons doing what they are ordinarily expected to do or at times for keeping the oath of office to which they swore?

The answer is simple. These people stamped value on themselves by exhibiting a quality which has become very rare in our world today irrespective of our religious inclinations.

This quality is called INTEGRITY. It is now a very rare virtue in our society, even in the places you would expect it to be the norm.

Many people and scholars have given INTEGRITY different definitions depending on the perspective from which they are looking at it. But the Encata dictionary gives INTEGRITY three definition which I summarize thus:

1. Possession of firm principles: the quality of possessing and steadfastly adhering to high moral principles or professional standards.

2. Completeness: the state of being complete or undivided.

3. Wholeness: the state of being sound or undamaged.

Some teachers of God's Word have described INTEGRITY as a state of blamelessness, some say it is being consistently consistent. But whatever and however any scholar defines it, they all sum up to the same meaning.

Today, there is a severe and serious absence of integrity in the society, especially in leadership whether in secular or Christian leadership. It has become so devastating that some regard it as another form of AIDS. However, this time, this AIDS is not acquired immune-deficiency syndrome. It is rather called Acute Integrity Deficiency Syndrome.

It is so ravaging that it has made evangelism and winning of souls difficult in the Christian faith. In the secular world, especially in politics, it has caused total distrust and voter apathy among other things.

Integrity has become the missing link between what we say and what we do. It has become the missing link between the vision and the achievement. It has also become the missing link between the oath sworn to and the attitude exhibited. Integrity has further become the missing link between the character and the characteristics. In fact integrity has become the missing link between what is advertised and what is received. It is the missing link between the outward packaging and the real content of the packet.

A man's possession of integrity can be the door opener he needs to get to the highest heights in his chosen profession, career, business or political aspirations. On the other hand too, a man's lack of integrity can bring a disastrous downfall, a crash from the olympian height to a valley position .In many instances, peoples integrity. have proven to be of greater value than their resume.

In this book, we shall be looking at this all important subject of integrity from many perspectives as the Lord has directed and as He enables us. But special attention will be paid to leadership (especially Christian leadership).

01

THE WIDER VIEW OF INTEGRITY

Integrity should
be an integral part
of your everyday
life, when in the
secret or in the
open place.

One

CHAPTER ONE

THE WIDER VIEW OF INTEGRITY

In the introduction, I tried to give some dictionary definitions from the dictionary of the word integrity as follows:

a. Possession of firm principles

b. Completeness

c. Wholeness

d. Blamelessness

e. Consistently consistent

Indeed, one can summarily say that all the above definitions mean being disciplined and trustworthy.

Remember that the word, discipline, was coined from the word disciple. When you talk of disciple, you immediately remember the followers of our Lord and Saviour Jesus Christ during His sojourn here on planet earth.

They were called HIS DISCIPLES.

Who is a disciple? A disciple is someone who believes and helps to spread the doctrine of another. And it was because these disciples of Jesus Christ believed, and lived the life of Jesus Christ as well as spread His doctrine that they were for the first time called Christians in Antioch. The Bible says in Acts 11:26;"And when he had found him, he brought him unto Antioch. And it came to pass, that a whole year they assembled themselves with the church and taught much people. And the disciples were called Christians first in Antioch".

Why were they called Christians? It looked like a mockery in the beginning but the truth is that they called them CHRISTIANS because, their ways and manner of life were like those of Jesus Christ.

But even before then, in Act 4:12, though they did not call them Christians in this instance, people around them already noted that these men had indeed been greatly influenced by their mentor and master Jesus Christ.

> *"Now when they saw the boldness of Peter and John and perceived that they were unlearned and ignorant men, they marveled and they took knowledge of them that they had been with Jesus"* (Act 4:12).

What was it that they saw in these disciples and noted that they had been with Jesus and were behaving characteristically like Him? These men were disciplined, and trustworthy. They lived firmly by the principles their Master and mentor had practised. They never deviated from them. They preached what they were already practicing. (Act 1:1). They also were epitomes of what they preached.

Their yeah was their yeah, and their nay was their nay. They were indeed the Bible that their followers read in order to understand the ways of the Master.

That was why Paul could boldly tell the Philippian Christians in Phil. 4:9. "Those things which you have both learned, and received and heard, and seen in me, do and the God of peace shall be with you" (KJV).

Only a man who is sure. of his steadfastness, or a man of integrity can boldly instruct as Paul did. Let us go a step further to look at that statement from Paul' He said those things which you have LEARNED, and RECEIVED, and HEARD, and SEEN in me, do!

Those four words, learned, received, heard, seen, cover every area of Paul's activities. He was sure that whether it was by his modus operandi, or by modus preparandi or by modus Vivendi, everything he did was according to Christ's standard!

Therefore, following him whether by his teaching, or by his conversations, or by his appearances or by his activities, the church members would in no wise compromise their belief. He strictly adherred to the principles of the doctrine of Jesus Christ. That is integrity! .Paul was indeed an epitome of what it meant to be a disciple with the lifestyle of integrity.

Consider again a man like Job, he was an epitome of integrity. Even God Himself boasted about it to Satan. "And the Lord said unto Satan, hast thou considered my servant Job, that there is none like him in the earth, a perfect and an upright man, one that feareth God, and escheweth evil? And still he holdeth fast his INTEGRITY, although thou movedst me against him, to destroy him without cause"JOB.2:3 (KJV).

From this verse of scripture we can also have what we may call the expatiation of what integrity really means. And to do that well, let us look at how the New Living Translation (NLT) version puts Job 2:3.

Then the Lord asked Satan, "Have you noticed my servant Job? He is the finest man in all the earth. He is blameless, a man of complete integrity. He fears God and stays away from evil. And he has maintained his integrity, even though you urged me to harm him without cause" (NLT).

So we can adduce from the above that a man of integrity is one who:

- is blameless
- fears the Lord
- stays away from evil.

When you say that a man is blameless, you mean that he is without guilt. A man without guilt is of impeccable integrity. No matter how you investigate the accusations against him, you will discover that he is blameless. The accusations will crash like a pack of cards. You will easily discover his innocence, honesty and transparency.

The Bible says that the fear of the Lord is the beginning of wisdom (Ps. 111:10). Fear here means reverential fear. That is having respect for God. It is this respect for God that makes you to live blamelessly (that is, innocently, honestly and transparently). This respect and honour is also what makes you to stay away from evil and, even the appearance of it. Even when you are in a very difficult situation you still decide to maintain your honesty and transparence. That is what the scripture called the integrity of the upright. Proverb 11:3 says, “the integrity of the upright shall guide them, but the perverseness of transgressors shall destroy them (KJV).

Integrity, indeed, guides and preserves. That was why when Job's wife asked him after he had been terribly afflicted, and even buffeted by Satan, “Dost thou still retain thine integrity? Curse God, and die” (Job 2:9). Job answered and said “Thou speakest as one of the foolish women speaketh, what? Shall we receive good at the hand of God, and shall we not receive evil”? (Job 2:10). But we know that the evil did not come from God!

Job continued by saying “Though He slay me, yet will I trust in Him: but I will maintain mine own ways before Him. He also shall be my salvation; for an hypocrite shall not come before Him”. (Job 13:15-16).

Integrity will always keep you focused in the right direction, help you make the right decisions and overcome every affliction or temptation.

There is something we must understand from Job. He said "though He slay me" He meant that even if God killed him, he (Job) will still trust that He (God) must have done the right thing! Job was a man who truly understood or knew the God he worshipped – that there is no wrong doing in Him. God Himself is integrity epitomized! Job also understood that whatever decision God took concerning us was the best for us because it was always in our best interest. Jeremiah 29:11 says "For I know the thoughts that I think toward you, saith the Lord, thoughts of peace, and not evil, to give you an expected end". If we can understand the ways of God, no temptation or trial will overwhelm us. Daniel 11:32[6] says "But the people who know their God shall be strong, and do exploit" and I hereby add that on the contrary, the people who do not know their God shall be weak and be exploited!

To be strong is to have absolute trust in God despite your situation. You know He will always turn it around. God did exactly that for Job. Job 42:10 says "And the Lord turned the captivity of Job, when he prayed for his friends; also the Lord gave Job twice as much as he hard before". Integrity will always be rewarded, and handsomely, too.

Another point that I must not fail to bring out from Job 13:16 is "For an hypocrite shall not come before Him" .There is a lot of hypocrisy in our society. There is also what I may call "Hypocritical integrity. We pretend to exude integrity – that is – as much as the eye can see in the open. We feign integrity when everything is going well with us, and there are no pressures. We feign honesty and transparency when we are targeting something, like an appointment, a promotion, or a favour. But when we have achieved our purpose, we now showcase our true colour. There is something William Shakes**peare** said in the book Julius Caesar. He says "Lowliness is the young ambitions ladder, whereby the climber, upward, turns his back to the base degrees by which he did ascend" .For some of us hypocritical integrity is but a ladder to achieve a purpose or an aim. We use it as a means to an end. As it is said, the end justifies the means.

This is much exhibited by politicians, who relate even with the lowest of the low in society, make donations and become emergency philantropists during campaigns so as to appear eligible for election. But meet them as soon as election is over and they have assumed office, you will see different persons altogether. Their true nature emerges. When you see or hear of the evils or atrocities they commit, you will now realize that ab initio, there was no integrity or humility. It was all pretense. This attitude of pretentious or feigned integrity is not only the attitude of politicians but it is also very present in the life of believers. I have had opportunity of being close to seminarians or student pastors of different denominations. While in training those of them whose intentions are to use priesthood as a profession, but not as a divine calling will pretentiously appear to show a life of honesty or transparency, even the fear of the Lord. This is only to enable them complete the program. They are just like wolves in sheep's clothing.

But as they complete the program, their true pictures will emerge. They will be involved in all manner of vices: adultery, embezzlement of funds, drunkenness and total disobedience to their superiors.

Integrity should be an integral part of your everyday life, when in the secret or in the open place. Whether it is noticeable or not. It does not matter whether you are under pressure or not. Even when you are going to pay dearly for taking the stand. Especially for you, who professes to be a Christian. Integrity should not be an optional virtue, because our Master whom we are supposed to be emulating while He was on earth was integrity epitomized, and remains more so even in eternity.

It should manifest in everything you do It affects the way you talk, the way you work, the way you relate, the way you rule, the way you serve, even the way you dress, drink and eat. It is an all encompassing thing. Integrity is not a seasonal or circumstantially determined way of behaviour but it is rather an internalized and perpetual way of life for all times till eternity.

Integrity does not however mean that you cannot make mistakes or wrong judgements. No, but it is in fact a show of integrity that when you make mistakes or wrong judgements, you accept or acknowledge it, and take steps to make corrections or amendments as necessary. If you need to apologize to those affected by the mistake or wrong judgement, you do so from the heart and without delay.

02

INTEGRITY IN THE SECRET PLACE

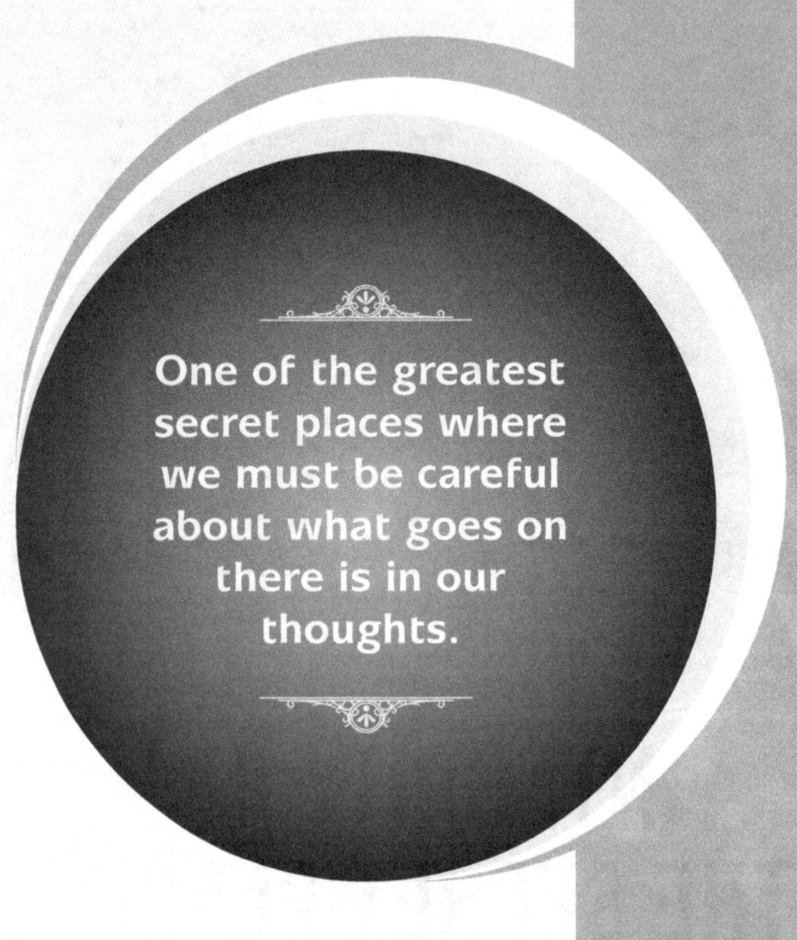
One of the greatest
secret places where
we must be careful
about what goes on
there is in our
thoughts.

Two

CHAPTER TWO

INTEGRITY IN THE SECRET PLACE

In the previous chapter, I described what I called hypocritical integrity. It is like a make belief showmanship and acting. There is nothing true about it

However, the knowledge and practice of the truth is what establishes a believer or any person as a man of integrity. Integrity manifests in what a person does in the secret place where no eyes are prying to see. Or where even if they pry, they will succeed in seeing nothing.

When we talk of secret place, it could be in the confines of your house or office where you are alone. It could be in the privacy of your consulting room as a Clinician. It could be in your office as a manager or chief executive officer, it could be in your manufacturing company, your accounting firm, or wherever you are doing your business. It could also be in that place where you are meeting to strategize with your cohorts.

The actions or decisions you take in such places go a long way to show of what stuff you are indeed made. They portray your personality and your secret thoughts. They, above all, show the extent of the fear of the Lord that is in you.

Take as an example the story of Joseph (Jacob's beloved son that was sold into slavery by his brothers out of jealousy) in Potiphar's house. We were told in Genesis 39:7-9, that his master's wife Mrs Potiphar, kept disturbing him, asking him to come and lie (that is have sexual relationship) with her, but he consistently refused.

"And it came to pass after these things, that his master's wife cast her eyes upon Joseph; and she said, lie with me. But he refused, and said unto his master's wife. Behold my master wotteth not what is with me in the house, and he hath committed all that he hath to my hand. There is none greater in this house than 1; neither hath he kept back anything from me but thee, because thou art his wife; how can I do this great wickedness and sin against God? (v7-9).

If, this incident happened in the present day, the story would that have been a great opportunity for Joseph to "make it". It would have been a great opportunity for him to domestically overthrow Potiphar, to get riches, and to even secure his release from being a house boy that is, and be elevated to a higher office. To a charlatan, or an opportunist, it would have been an answered prayer, not minding that it was adultery. But being a man of integrity, Joseph told his master's wife that he had been so well respected and trusted by Potiphar, and therefore he could not afford to betray the trust for any reason. He was saying, I am so far grateful and even overwhelmed by the level of trust and respect my master has for me already, I will be greedy to ask for anything more. Can I tell you something? A greedy man cannot be a man of integrity!

A man of integrity always displays an attitude of gratitude, with godliness and contentment which the Bible says is great gain (1 Tim 6:6). Examine what Joseph said in v9 "...how can I do this great wickedness, and sin against God?

Joseph was not only considering the fact that it was a great display of betrayal of trust to Potiphar who trusted him and committed so much into his hands, but above all, he saw it as wickedness and sin against God! A man of integrity recognizes that there is God to whom all of us are eventually accountable, even if no man discovers our wrong doings here and now.

This is indeed of paramount importance to all who desire to live a godly life of integrity here on earth; that even if men do not see your good works, or even the bad ones, that the omnipresent God sees all things, whether they are done in the open or in the secret.

Hebrew 4:13 says "Neither is there any creature that is not manifest in His sight; but all things are naked and opened unto the eyes of Him with whom we have to do"

Ps. 139:7-11 says "Whither shall I go from thy spirit? Or whither shall I flee from thy presence? If I ascend up into heaven, thou art there; if I make my bed in hell, behold, thou art there. If I take the wings of the morning, and dwell in the uttermost parts of the sea; even there shall thy hand lead me, and thy right hand shall hold me. If I say, surely the darkness shall cover me; even the night shall be light about me. Yea, the darkness hideth not from thee; but the night shineth as the day; the darkness and the light are both alike to thee".

Our God sees in secret. Matthew's gospel put it this way ".... thy father which seeth in secret himself shall reward thee openly (Matt. 6:4). So even when no man, nor even your lieutenants and colleagues appreciate your display of integrity, do not be discouraged because there is some one who sees, both in the light and in the dark. He will surely reward you in due time. I say this because sometimes when you decide to apply integrity in situations, some who do not understand this see you as being excessively strict or unnecessarily unco-operative.

Now remember, we are talking about integrity in the secret place, using Joseph as a good example.

Verse 11 of Genesis 39 is very instructive. Hear what it says "And it came to pass about this time that Joseph went into the house to do his business; and there was none of the men of the house there within. And she caught him by his garment, saying lie with me; and he left his garment in her hand, and fled, and got him out".

Note: "and there was none of the men of the house there within". This is purely in the secret place! Joseph, if he was ab intio pretentious or hypocritical about his integrity stance would have succumbed at this time. After all, nobody was there to see and report to Potiphar what transpired between him and Mrs Potiphar. But Joseph resisted her tempting overtures and fled.

Yes, indeed, there are times we must need to "flee" so as to maintain our integrity. Even though, the adulterous woman caught and ceased his garment and used it as an evidence against him, and this eventually landed him in prison,but do not forget that it was from this prison that his ability to interpret dreams was discovered! That was after he accurately interpreted the dreams of the Baker and the Butler. When Pharaoh had a dream which none of his wise men could interpret, the chief butler remembered how Joseph had accurately interpreted the dream that restored him to his job. Joseph was sought for. I guess you know the rest of the story that it was from interpreting Pharaoh's dream that he was promoted from prisoner to prime minister – the second most powerful person in Egypt then, only second to Pharaoh himself. This is what integrity can do. A lot of times, a life of integrity looks like you are swimming against the tide, but ultimately you will be remembered, rewarded, received and promoted. Indeed, the devil may plot against you using human agents, either to discourage or distract you, but if you remain resilient, you will discover that the plot of the enemy will indeed quicken the plan of God for your life.

Just think about it, let us suppose Joseph had yielded to the lustful Mrs Potiphar. That would have ended the plan of God for his life and all that dream of being ahead and above his brothers. Suppose Job had yielded to his wife's suggestion, to forget this integrity issue, curse God and die,(Job.2:9), where would Job be now or what would his recovery have been like.

Have not many of us missed our days of visitation or the purpose of God for our lives because of lack of integrity in the secret place. Thank God, we have a God of second chance. Maybe, if you can right now pause a little and ask Him for forgiveness (as I have done), I believe He will do it.

One of the greatest secret places where we must be careful about what goes on there is in our thoughts. Proverb 23:7 says "for as he thinketh in his heart, so is he (KJV).

If we do not actively, with the word of God suppress and expunge some of the thoughts that go through our minds or hearts, we may consciously or unconsciously begin to act accordingly. That is why it is said that we may not stop the bird from flying over our heads, but we must stop or prevent them from nesting on our heads.

Several reasons and circumstances may cause all sorts of thought to come to our minds, but we must not hesitate to rebuke every evil thought immediately, even verbally, I do it always. Also use the word of God which is quick and powerful to cancel and counteract evil unprofitable thoughts. Apostle Paul calls it "Casting down imaginations, and every high thing that exalteth itself against the knowledge of God, and bringing into captivity every thought to the obedience of Christ"(2Cor.10:5)

Indeed, it is more of an active thing than a passive thing. Didn't the Bible say, "Resist the devil and he will flee from you (Jam. 4:7). In fact when we insist, the devil will desist. We must resist him, not only in the physical, but also in our thoughts or minds and hearts. Paul also admonishes us thus: "finally, brethren whatsoever things are true, whatsoever things are just, whatsoever things are pure, whatsoever things are lovely, whatsoever things are of good report, if there be any virtue, and if there by any praise, think on these things" (Phil.4:8;KJV).

Paul gave this powerful advice above because he knew or understood how powerful our thoughts can be. There are greater and unimaginable extents to which what we think or nurture in our hearts can affect us, even afflict us. There is what we call pseudocyesis in medical practice.

PSEUDO means false while CYESIS means pregnancy. Some women who are in the reproductive age and who after marriage are yet to get pregnant, especially, when the period of waiting is extended can experience pseudocyesis. Their bodies begin to show signs and symptoms of pregnancy; they miss their monthly menses (amenorrhoea), their breasts begin to get bigger, even the abdomen begins to distend! When you see them, you will think they are pregnant, but examination shows that the womb (uterus) is empty! Their bodies are acting in according with the thoughts or wishes of their hearts.

The same thing we notice in pseudocyesis also happens in persons (or patients) who we call hypochondriacs. These are patients who always present with imaginary symptoms and signs of ailments. When you clerk or examine them as a physician, you cannot elicit the symptoms or signs (and ailments) they are constantly complaining about. It is all in their minds (or thoughts). It is called hypochondriasis, that is, chronic and abnormal anxiety about imaginary symptoms and ailments.

Sorry if I have stretched you too far into the field of medicine (my professional field). I was only trying to emphasise how powerful the secret place of the mind can be, and the drastic changes it can bring to our lives. That is why the Bible says that we must cast down imaginations. Don't ever underestimate it. When the Bible uses the word CAST DOWN, it implies the use of some force, applying conscious effort to overcome. It is not something to be done perfunctorily. That is why I said earlier that sometimes you will need to verbalize your counteracting statement, if it is in prayer, it needs to be fervent and effectual.

> *The Lord Himself makes it clear in Luke 6:45 that "A good man out of the good treasure of his heart bringeth forth that which is good, and an evil man out of the evil treasure of his heart bringeth forth that which is evil: for of the abundance of the heart his mouth speaketh" (KJV)*
>
> *Here, I am particularly interested in the last portion of the verse("for of the abundance of the heart his mouth speaketh"). Speaketh here does not only mean speaking as in talking, it also means acting or doing. So for a man of integrity, his display of integrity actually begins from the contents or thoughts of his heart. He is first convinced in his heart of what is the right thing to do, then he puts it into practice. Look at this in Daniel. 1:8 "But Daniel purposed*

in his heart that he would not defile himself with the portion of the king's meat, nor with the wine which he drank: therefore he requested of the prince of the eunuch's that he might not defile himself (KJV).

Daniel first PURPOSED IN HIS HEART not to eat the portion of the king's food or drink the wine, then he went ahead to inform the eunuch of his decision, that is, he carried out what he had decided in his heart

I have emphasized so much on the secret place, whether it is the secret place of our hearts and thoughts, or the secret place where we are alone and concealed from prying eyes, that is our privacy because this is one place our adversory, the devil attacks us a lot. And here, our vulnerability is high if we are not alert. Can you recall what the devil suggested to you sometime ago when you were alone with that lady in your office or hotel room.? Can you remember what the enemy whispered to you when you were alone counting either the church offering which was big even when you were in a serious financial need? What of the day you were trusted to go and make purchases for that institution or company running into hundreds of thousands or even millions? When you eventually got them at lesser prices than budgeted, and you had balance, what did you do? You remember that if eventually you honestly returned the balance, that there was a suggestion that you should have used the money for yourself. That victory you had was because you decided to retain your integrity. If on the other hand you failed to return the balance, but used it for personal things, you had yielded to the trap the enemy set for in the secret place. You became vulnerable. You could not retain your integrity. STOP BRIEFLY AND PRAY AND ASK FOR FORGIVENESS AND IF POSSIBLE MAKE RESTITUTION.

Today we have many believers who are addicted to pornography or masturbation in their privacies. Others may be practicing lesbianism or homosexuality in the private place.

Remember that one of the definitions of integrity is possession of firm principles. As Christians, there are firm principles for the practice of our day to day Christianity which are entrenched in the word of God. If you are indeed a principled man/woman, that is, a man/woman of integrity, you have no business practicing either masturbation, lesbianism or even homosexuality. There should be no reason on earth for this, even if you are under any form of pressure. That pressure cannot be compared with what Joseph suffered in Potiphar's house. You are therefore inexcusable.

Maybe, one thing that will help us all is to remind ourselves always that with God, there is nothing like a secret place. Remember, *"All things are naked and opened unto the eyes of Him with whom we have to do" (Roman 4:13).* If this can sink into our hearts, we will be more rational both in our thoughts and in our actions. And as many as are conscious of making heaven, we better be well guided.

03

INTEGRITY IN LEADERSHIP

A leader at whatever level, circular or spiritual, that lacks integrity is like a blind man who is leading the way.

Three

CHAPTER THREE

INTEGRITY IN LEADERSHIP

In Rom.2:17-24, the Apostle Paul writes "Behold, thou at called a Jew, and restest in the law, and makest thy boast of God, and knowest His will, and approvest the things that are more excellent, being instructed out of the law; and art confident that thou thyself art a guide of the blind, a light of them which are in darkness, an instructor of the foolish, a teacher of babes, which hast the form of knowledge and of the truth in the law.

> *Thou therefore which teachest another, teachest thou not thyself? Thou that preachest a man should not steal, doest thou steal? Thou that sayest a man should not commit adultery, dost thou commit adultery? Thou that abhorest idols, does thou commit sacrilege? Thou that makest thy boast of the law, dishonorest thou God?*
>
> *For the name of God is blasphemed among the Gentiles through you, as it is written"(KJV)*

The Jews in the Biblical times (and probably today) were so proud and boasted of the fact that they knew God, His laws and methods more than other people (then Gentiles).Well that was because they were the chosen people or the nation of God, whose patriarch, heard from God directly and received His statutes and ordinances. Seeing themselves as the custodians of the law, they were naturally teachers of the law and as such the leaders of the people in the things of God. So, they were always in a position to teach, to rebuke, and to insist that people acted and lived in accordance with the tenets of the law. This was the stock in trade of the Jewish sect called the Pharisees who were noted for strict adherence to Jewish traditions. The other sect that also did that were the scribes (the journalist or writers in their midst). These were among the foremost leaders of the Jews. However, the Bible in Matt. 23:1-5 says about them *"Then spake Jesus to the multitude, and to his disciples saying, the Scribes sit in Moses seat: All therefore whatsoever they bid your observe, that observe and do; but do not ye after their works: for they say, and do not for they bind heavy burdens and grievous to be borne, and lay then on men's shoulders, but they themselves will not move them with one of their fingers. But all their works they do for to be seen of men: they make broad their phylacteries, and enlarge the borders of their garments"*. (KJV).

The account that Jesus gave here concerning the scribes and Pharisees can only be likened to what I had earlier called hypocritical integrity. In many scriptural passages, Jesus addressed them as hypocrites. They only honoured God with their mouth, but their hearts were far away from God. They never made any effort to keep the laws, and ordinances they insisted that other people (their subordinates) should keep or follow. Their ways of life completely negated their instruction. Theirs was, "do as I say, but not as I do"!

Their lives were a complete contradiction to what they taught. That was why Paul asked those rhetorical questions in Rom. 2:21-23: that which you teach others to do, do you do it? That also which you teach or instruct your subordinates to avoid, or not to do, do you also avoid them or do you also not do them?

How can you preach against stealing, yet you are a thief! How can you preach against adultery, but you are an adulterer? Then, where is your integrity? It is like the medical doctor who advises his patients against smoking in his consulting clinic. But moments after leaving the clinic, he goes to smoke, and what if the patient he had advised moments ago against it sees him smoking. Do you think that the patient will ever take that advice seriously? No, of course!

What do you think of a Pastor or Reverend gentleman, who comes to the pulpit and preaches against adultery, but it is an open and proven secret that he has a "mistress" in the church, who is not his wife, but indeed the wife of one of his members?

What do you think of a Chief Executive Officer (CEO), or a manager in a bank or any other institution who parades himself to be a believer and in fact has established a fellowship or a prayer meeting in the company where he preaches about uprightness or righteousness, yet he is known to be defrauding the company in many ways, or if in the bank, he is known as a conduct pipe through which politicians are siphoning the State or the peoples money away to their personal and foreign accounts?

These are all leaders who are leading without integrity. Their type of leadership can only be called whited sepulchres. Whoever follows or emulates their ways of leadership will meet a waterloo in the end. But Paul, the Apostle, a man or leader with integrity says in Phil. 4:9, "*Those things which ye have both learned and received, and heard and seen in me, do and the God of peace shall be with you*".

A true leader leads by example. He should be a practitioner of what he instructs others to do. The book of Acts of apostles chapter one, verse one (Acts 1:1) says "*The former treatise have I made, O Theophilus, of all that Jesus began both to do and teach (KJV).*

Note carefully, Jesus began both to do and teach. That is, the Lord Himself began, first, to do them before He began to teach them. You can even also put it the other way round, He operated or behaved in accordance with His teachings.

One of the biggest problems we have in our country today is the dearth of leaders who lead by example. Here in our country, Nigeria, the truth is that the makers of the law are also the greatest breakers of the law. We live in a country were stealing, and all forms of corrupt practices have become the order of the day. Right from the era of our independence from our colonial masters in 1960 till date, it has been the same and, in fact, it has been growing in geometrical progression. The reason for the first military coup in 1966 that removed the government of Dr Nnamdi Azikiwe and Alhaji Tafawa Belewa was primarily corruption in high places. But during the years of the military junta that spanned up to three decades which was characterized by coups and counter coups, corruption continued to increase. Each group of military officers removing the ones in power apparently with the same excuse of corrupt leadership. Why was it so? Simply because, even though they came flaunting themselves as officers of integrity, it was all hypocritical. They were as corrupt as those they removed. Even when civilian administrations occasionally replaced the military, it was no better. Those men and women, whether in uniforms or otherwise have succeeded in raping the economy of Nigeria and have left empty treasuries. A nation that once boasted that money is not the problem, but what to do with money cannot today pay salaries of workers. Even the pensioners, men and women that have served their fatherland meritoriously with their youth and the best and vibrant years of their lives, are dying of hunger and lack. That is what lack of integrity could do to a people.

Whereas many of those military officers (now retired) and politicians are living in opulence, with a mindless display of ostentatious living and conspicuous consumption. They build their houses with imported sand, drink imported water and drive the costliest cars, the poor masses of this country even in this 21st century drink mosquito infested pond water, live in leaking thatched houses without any form of infrastructure at all, and have only narrow meandering bush paths connecting their villages. This is what you see in almost all African countries because of leadership that is bereft of integrity. There is abject poverty in the land. The wise man in Prov. 29:2 says "*When the righteous are in authority, the people rejoice; but when the wicked beareth rule, the people mourn" (KJV).*

Those who have held the reins of power in Nigeria have been desperately wicked. This abject poverty is in the midst of plenty. Yes, plenty; most African countries are blessed (some say cursed) with almost all sorts of mineral deposits like Uranium, diamond, gold, oil, bauxite, iron ore, arable farmland, wonderful seasons of the year, just name it. But what have we done with them? Nigeria has almost all mineral deposits that one could name. Indeed some are yet to be tapped or touched. But we are counted as one of the poorest countries in the world. That reminds me of a funny, but yet intelligent story one of my professors of psychiatry, in the medical school told us. He said that when God was creating the world, in some countries he put just a few mineral deposits, in some He did not put any at all. But when He was creating Nigeria, He put all sorts of mineral deposits in large quantities and His angels asked Him, Daddy why are you doing this in Nigeria? And He answered them and said, wait and see the type of human beings I am going to put there! As funny as the story sounds, is it not very instructive? Human beings that have no integrity!!

Civilization started in Egypt (Africa). The first university in the world was in Egypt. But where is Egypt today in world affairs? Can Egypt stand to be counted except for corruption and violence. All these are products of leadership that lacks integrity.

Today, another example of leadership without integrity in African is the sit-tight governments syndrome. Some African leaders want to remain presidents for life. Some have stayed more than four decades in rulership. They remain in office even when they are very old, incompetent and have run down the economies of their countries.

Once they come into governance, they change their national constitution to entrench the perpetuation of themselves in government. Even when it causes violence and death of the citizens,(like is currently happening in Burundi), they send the army and police to kill and brutalize the citizens they are supposed to be serving to better their lives. They get many killed, and others are imprisoned for demanding good governance. Others run and seek asylum in other nations. The irony is that some of the leaders doing these things were once in opposition even in the bush fighting what they called despotic and dictatorial governments. President Yoweri Museveni of Uganda is one such example. At a certain time, he claimed to be a believer! But see what is happening in Uganda now. He has been Ugandan president since 29th January 1986 till now (2023) that is for more than thirty six years already. Yet, he was a man who fought the governments of both Milton Obete and Idi Amin.

What of Robert Gabriel Mugabe; born 21 February

1924 was the president of Zimbabwe from 22nd December 1987 till 21st November 2017,a record 30years even at the age of 93years! He died on 6th September 2019 at age 95. He was initially elected as Prime Minister, head of government, in 1980, and served in that office until 1987 when he became the country's first executive head of State. At 93years of age, he was still clinging to power tenaciously, despite the economic devastation he had brought to his country. Even despite obvious signs of senility.

This is the kind of leaders Africa is unfortunate to have, both living and dead; Mobutu Sese Seko, military dictator and president of the democratic republic of the Congo from 1965 to 1997 (32yrs); Muammar Gaddafi ruled Libya from 1969 to 2011 (42yrs), before he was killed, Paul Biya of Cameroun has been president of that country from 6th November 1982 (40 years plus) till now (2023). The list is endless. These men completely under developed their countries and by extrapolation, Africa. And when you examine the style of leadership of any of the above, living or dead, you will discover that they lacked integrity. They perpetuated themselves in government by suppressing the opposition, assassinations, imprisonments, rigging elections, amassing wealth corruptly, and settling and bribing their sycophants or followers. Some of them acquired personal riches greater than that of their countries, or that of some African countries put together.

It is this chronic and persistent absence of integrity in leadership that has kept Africa in darkness and under developed. It has remained the third world perpetually. And instead of moving forward to the second world it is lapsing backward to the fourth world. Today, the sit-tight leaders and their mal-administration have brought sequella – wars, terrorism, militancy in these countries. We have such terrorist groups as the Al-shabaab, arising from Somalia and ravaging many countries. We have others like the Lord's Army of Uganda, now Boko Haram of Nigeria afflicting and devastating countries like Nigeria, Mali, Chad, Cameroun. We have the militants of the Niger Delta in Nigeria blowing up pipelines. We have had or still have devastating wars in Somalia, Liberia, Ivory Coast, Nigeria, Sierra Loan, Central African Republic, Congo DR, Libya and others.

This is what lack of integrity in leadership can cause a people, whether it is a country, community or even the church of Jesus Christ. Even here in our country Nigeria, the church has not been spared these internal wranglings and divisions because of lack of integrity in leadership. The Methodist Church of Nigeria had a protracted internal war that divided and devastated it. Thank God it was patched up after more than ten years, but the scars still remain. How would John and Charles Wesley feel if they were to come back alive and see what lack of integrity has done to their legacy. It has happened in The Apostolic Church, and that has factionalized it perpetually.

The most current is the ongoing fight for supremacy in the Assemblies of God Church Nigeria (AG) that has also factionalized it. The case is currently in the supreme court of Nigeria now waiting for adjudication. But see what the Bible says about going to court with your brother to judge spiritual things:

Writing to the Corinthians, Apostle Paul says "*Dare any of you, having a matter against another, go to law before the unjust, and not before the saints? Do you not know that the saints shall judge the world? And if the world shall be judged by you, are ye unworthy to judge the smallest matters? Know ye not that we shall judge angels? How much more things that pertains to this life?*

If then ye have judgments of things pertaining to this life, set them to judge who are least, esteemed in the church . I speak to your shame. Is it so, that there is not a wise man among you? No, not one that shall be able to judge between his brethren?

But brother goeth to law with brother, and that before the unbelievers. Now therefore there is utterly a fault among you, because ye go to law one with another. Why do ye not rather take wrong? Why do ye not rather suffer yourselves to be defrauded?"(1 Cor. 6:1-7)

But when you go to our courts today, from the magistrate court to the Supreme Court, they are inundated with all sorts of cases emanating from churches and fellowships. Majority of these cases are either as a result of lack of integrity in leadership which manifest as greed, financial mismanagement, favoritism, unconstitutional acts or a desire to overstay in tenureship, and using unconstitutional means to prolong your stay. In fact in some instances it originated from the flawed process of the selection of that leader.

But these squabbles are most painful and ridiculous when it emanates from the church of Jesus Christ. The Bible talks about the qualities of a leader, be it a bishop or an elder in Titus 1:7-9.

"For a bishop must be blameless as the steward of God; not self-willed, not soon angry, not given to wine, no striker, not given to filthy lucre, but a lover of hospitality, a lover of good men, a sober, just, holy, temperate; holding fast the faithful word he hath been taught, that we must be able by sound doctrine both to exhort and to convince the gainsayers.

Remember that in our introduction, one of the adjectives we used to define integrity is blamelessness. How many of today's leaders, be they bishops, general overseers, general superintendents, presidents, prelates, presbyters or whatever nomenclature that is used, are blameless.

The New International Version (NIV) describes a leader thus: *"Not given to filthy lucre" as "not pursuing dishonest gain".* Many leaders in the church of Jesus Christ have been overtaken by the spirit of mammon because of their quest for dishonest gains. They lie, they manipulate figures, they embark on frivolous projects just to embezzle money. Some of them merchandise prayers. The amount or type of prayer one gets depends on what one can pay. They now sale "anointed" olive oils of different gradations.

Talking about lying, a nurse who worked with me in my department told us a story. She said that her husband was the treasurer of their church. One Sunday night, armed robbers came to their home, and stole a lot of things at gun point. Her husband is a successful businessman. Fortunately, for him, though the robbers took away a lot of things including money from their home, they were not able to see the church money where he kept it. So it was safe. In the morning when the church pastor came to their house to sympathize with them over what happened, the man elatedly told the pastor that the church money was spared, and was still intact. The pastor was happy but suggested to the treasurer that he should inform the church council that the money was also stolen. So that in the end the two of them could share it!

Does it look like fiction to you? No, it is real. Have you heard what some bishops or ministers in collusion with building committees do with building funds. The building never ever gets completed. More than thrice the amount that should have been used to complete them have already been spent. But when you investigate, you find that the reverend minister and committee members have all during that period built new private houses in choice areas.

Haggai in chapter 1:7-10 says "*Thus saith the Lord of hosts; consider your ways. Go up to the mountain, and bring wood, and build the house; and I will take pleasure in it, and I will be glorified, saith the Lord. Ye looked for much, and lo, it came to little; and when ye brought it home, I did blow upon it. Why? Said the Lord of hosts. Because of nine house that is waste, and ye run every man unto his own house. Therefore the heaven over you stayed from dew, and the earth is stayed from her fruit*".

The above scripture is saying that because you have not raised money to build a befitting house for the Lord, therefore you will be punished for it! What do you think will be the fate of those who misappropriated the money others contributed to construct the building. It will be more than the heaven over them being stayed from dew and the earth being stayed from fruit. That is why we are being warned to consider our ways.

Many leaders because of lack of integrity in leadership end up with curses for themselves and their families instead of the blessings that should come from serving Him blamelessly.

The bible says that God is a rewarder of them that diligently seek (or serve) Him (Heb. 11:6).

In Heb. 6:10, it says *"For God is not unrighteous to forget your work and labour of love, which ye have showed toward His name, in that ye have ministered to the saints, and do minister".*

May be, that is why David said in Ps 37:25, *"I have been young, and now am old; yet I have not seen the righteous forsaken, nor his seed begging bread".*

A leader, whether in the spiritual or secular realm who leads with integrity, can never go unrewarded both here in this life and in eternity.

On the other hand, take note of what the Bible says about making money by unrighteous means: Jere. 17:11 says

> *"As the partridge sitteth on eggs, and hatcheth them not; so he that getteth riches, and not by right, shall leave them in the midst of his days and at his end shall be a fool".*

One of the sure ways to incur premature death for yourself and sometimes for your lineage is to get riches by all sorts of crooked means. There is so much pursuit of dishonest gain in the work of ministry today. Ministers now lie in the name of God saying that God spoke to them. I heard a story a young man told of a man of God. He said that on this particular Sunday their pastor announced that there was going to be Holy Communion service in church that day. And the young man was happy and eager to participate in it. After all, the Bible says as often as you drink it, you do it in the remembrance of Him. (1 Cor. 11:25-26). After all other things the "man of God" said including being in a pure state to partake in it and the fact that it will bring healing, which are all true; he now suddenly said after a pause, the Lord has just told me that those who will partake in this holy communion will only be those who sew a substantial seed for it! Beloved is that scriptural? Is it not obtaining by trick (OBT,,a.k.a 419)!

And there are so many similar things going on in the church of Jesus Christ today. All in the bid to extort money from unsuspecting, innocent, but most especially gullible and desperate members.

All sort of title are being bestowed on members today, with funny names, as if it is chieftaincy title in the church. In every case and situation you must donate something (especially money) to the church. In the villages when they perceive that your children are presumably well to do, they invite you for an award. The target is not you but your children.

What is happening now is almost like what happened some centuries ago when the Catholic Church invented the doctrine of purgatory and the infallibility of the Pope. Then, they created indulgences and sold them as a means to pay off the excessive debt that one Pope had incurred. The people were taught that if they spent enough money for an indulgence, then the clergy could grant them entrance into heavens. In fact, then, there was a legend that said that if a child died before its parents could pay for the baptism, the child was doomed to roam the earth as a firefly or some other bug or beast.

This is the kind of heresy the church leadership that lacks integrity teach their congregation just because it was looking for ways of extorting money from the membership in order to personally enrich themselves.

What else, but greed could have led these church leaders into these lies and heresies?

No wonder the Bible says in 1 Tim. 6:10 that, "*For the love of money is the root of all evil which while some coveted after they have erred from the faith and pierced themselves through with many sorrows*"

Such church leaders, be they addressed as Reverends, Pastors, Apostles, General overseers or even Pope who can fabricate such fables or tell such lies have indeed erred from the faith. Such men/women are no longer heavenly minded, rather they desire to gain the whole world at the expense of their souls. They have been blinded by greed and pecuniary pursuits.

> "*For what shall it profit a man if he shall gain the whole world, and lose his own soul?* (Mk. 8:36,).

A leader at whatever level, circular or spiritual, that lacks integrity is like a blind man who is leading the way. All those he is leading will fall into the pit and potholes and in the end develop fractures and wounds. Some may even die from wounds they sustained from visionless leadership. This is exactly what is affecting the nation and the church today.

So, we see that the absence of integrity in leadership is central to all the ills in our society whether in the church or in the secular world. It is the cause of discontentment and uprisings in nations. It is the cause of coups and counter coups in underdeveloped nations. It is the cause of all sorts of insurgencies and terrorist activities in nations. It is the cause of wars.

The absence of integrity is also the cause of poverty and underdevelopment of nations. It is the reason or root cause of recessions or depressed economies. It is the cause of unemployment that is soaring high in nations leading to such ills as armed robbery, kidnappings, advanced fee fraud, even assassinations.

Lack of integrity in leadership is also the root cause of severe indebtedness of nations – where they borrow money for some well planned projects that will develop their economies, but never use the money for such. It is the same reason many states (as in Nigeria today) cannot pay workers salaries, and the pensions of retirees. This in turn leads to recurrent industrial actions and strikes by workers. And because workers are no longer sure of their pensions and gratuities when they retire, they begin to defraud and steal while in service to establish things or projects that will sustain them when they retire. It is a vicious cycle.

The same absence of integrity in leadership in the church of Jesus Christ has driven out the presence of the Holy Spirit of God from the church such that today there is hardly any manifestation of the gifts of the Holy Spirit in our churches. True miracles are rare. So people are now faking it or even using powers of darkness, I mean magical powers to obtain "miracles". Healings, prophesies, words of wisdom, words of knowledge, discerning of spirit, tongues and interpretation have completely disappeared from many congregation.

For the same reason, people come to church service with their problems and also go away with them. Some out of gullibility or desperation now go to seek help from the wrong places and thereby attracting more problems to themselves. See what the Bible says in Ps. 66:18. *"If I regard iniquity in my heart, the Lord will not hear me"*. See also 2 Tim. 2:19. *"Nevertheless the foundation of God standeth sure, having this seal, the Lord knoweth them that are His. And, let everyone that nameth the name of Christ depart from iniquity"*.

One who calls himself a man of God cannot be living in iniquity and expecting God to still use him for proper and authentic signs and wonders. If you are living in iniquity, you are spiritually dry. But we can only give out from our overflow! You talk about overflow when there is a fullness, not when there is dryness. It is the same lack of integrity in leadership that has caused all forms of internal wranglings, bickerings and strife in denominations. There is anger, there is bitterness, hatred, backbiting, slandering and more within congregations. How can the spirit of God move? The Spirit of God is the spirit of Love because God is love (1 John 4:8).

In the same vain, many denominations have experienced several divisions or splitting because of lack of integrity. Sometimes before this takes place, there will be fighting physically in the church, and the matter ends up in the court. This always affects the hearts of the worshipers, and prevents the church from achieving the main and primary essence of our worshipping God – making heaven!

But the nagging question is; what is integrity in leadership and is it achievable?

INTEGRITY IN LEADERSHIP

I would define integrity in leadership as insisting to consistently do things the right, approved and constitutional way, and refusing to compromise one's stand at all, irrespective of whatever exigencies or pressures with which one may be confronted.

Is it achievable? My answer will also be YES! When I say YES, don't think I am oblivious of societal pressures and other vicissitudes of life. No. That is why I said "irrespective of whatever exigencies or pressure...".

The issue is that you must begin from the beginning. What does that mean? Remember in Dan. 1:8, we read "but Daniel purposed in his heart that he would not defile himself with a portion of the king's meat".

Purposed in his heart means that he determined from the beginning, he decided from the onset what he would do and what he would not do. When we from onset make up our minds on what we would do, or not do, what we would accept or not, the direction we would go or not go, we would not hesitate or vacillate in taking decisions. It is most times our vacillation or hesitancy that gives a leeway to the devil and his cohorts to come in with different opinions that could sway us from the right and approved way. That was why when there was an option to choose between worshipping God and worshipping the golden image Nebuchadnezzar made, the three Hebrew children, Shadrach, Meshach, and Abednego, answered and said to the king, *"O Nebuchadnezzar, we are not careful to answer thee in this matter..."* (Dan. 3:16)

"Not careful" in this matter means, we are not going to vacillate or hesitate in making our opinion or decision made known to you. Or put in another form, they were saying there was nothing to go home to consider, in this matter, that their decisions were already made. "Our minds are already made up. We do not care about the consequences of our actions, no matter how grave they may be". Possibly, if they had started to deliberate on it, and possibly made consultations, contrary opinions to their decision could have come in and if such opinions became too persuasive, they could probably have chickened out of their decision and determination! People of integrity know that it is not everything that you take to the court of public opinion.

What of Abraham? When God instructed him (in Gen. 22:1-2) to take his son, his only son Isaac to go and make a burnt offering in the land of Moriah, he rose up early in the morning and left with Isaac his son, and two other young men for the sacrifice. It was most unlikely that he ever tried to confer with Sarah his wife. Of course, you and I know that it would have been too difficult, if not impossible, for

Sarah to agree. Her knowledge of it would have stopped that journey. In Galatian 1:15-16, Paul said that when it pleased God to call him to go to preach the gospel to the heathen, that he didn't have to consult with anybody (flesh and blood) but immediately left for Arabia. Hear him; *"But when it pleased God, who separated me from my mother's womb, and called me by his grace, to reveal his son in me, that I might preach Him among the heathen; immediately 1 conferred not with flesh and blood".*

If Paul had called those with him and told them what he received from the Lord, that is, that his lot was to go and be a preacher to the gentiles, he would definitely have received a lot of discouragement. Even as yet a young believer, they may have exaggerated the dangers he would face there which could have frightened and possibly stopped him.

Are we saying here that you should not at any time confer with either colleagues or contemporaries in making decisions? No! Not at all. Understand the spirit of the argument. We are only saying that there are times going into that will work negatively against you. Be wise!

Furthermore, to ensure that you are a leader that has integrity make up your mind to work in accordance with the established rules, regulation, statutes, ordinances, and biblical injunctions.

We must understand that as believers, the word of God – the Bible – is our surest guide. .Look at what the Bible says about Ezra in Ezra 7:10; *"For Ezra had prepared his heart to seek the law of the Lord and to do it, and to teach in Israel statutes and judgments"*. Ezra had the enormous task of going to Jerusalem to rebuild the house of God which was in ruins. That time Israel had been devastated because a lot of the people had been carried into captivity, and idol worshippers had been used to repopulate its cities. There was ungodliness and all forms of vices. The land was terribly polluted and all forms of evil overtook the land so it was a time that it was difficult to do things the right way. It could have been a good reason for anybody to keep integrity aside and act any how in leadership.

But not so for Ezra. He prepared his mind to do things the right and godly way as well as to teach it. There are three things that helped Ezra to achieve leadership by integrity which he exhibited in rebuilding the house of God;

He decided to seek the law; that is to study the law. He knew that he needed to be conversant with the law (statutes and ordinances). Apostle Paul in 2Tim. 2:15 instructs; "*Study to show thyself approved unto God, a workman that needeth not to be ashamed, rightly dividing the word of truth"*.

A lot of leaders have made a shipwreck of their leadership because of their ignorance of the laws or statutes of their establishments. That way, they make themselves pawns in the hands of dubious colleagues and contemporaries who use them to achieve their dubious desires. Remember when the devil tempted our Master and Saviour Jesus Christ. On each occasion, the devil twisted the word and wanted Him to act wrongly. But the Lord kept telling him; "it is written!" How would He have known what was written, if He never studied it or had knowledge of the word. Hosea 4:6 says; my people are destroyed for lack of knowledge.

In the same way, a lot of Christian leaders, including ministers of the gospel preach heresy because of lack of the knowledge of the word. A true minister of the gospel or leader should have an in-depth knowledge of the word to give quality leadership. There are no two ways about it!

The second thing is that Ezra said, that he prepared his heart to seek the law of the Lord AND TO DO IT.(Ezra 7:10)

James 1:22, says; *"But be ye doers of the word and not hearers only, deceiving your own selves" (KJV)*. Ezra made up his mind to do according to the law. Remember what I said about Daniel and the other Hebrew children. Your decision from the onset matters a lot. It will help you achieve integrity in leadership and act in accordance with the law. You will never be led astray. You will be happy you did, and there are blessings that go with it.

Ezra also did something else "And to teach in Israel statutes and ordinances (Judgments)". He decided that he will also make the people he was leading knowledgeable in the statutes and ordnances of the land. He had to carry them along, otherwise whatever he was doing would look strange to them. They would possibly begin to oppose him and deliberately cripple his leadership. If they are not in the know, they will not be in the flow. If they are knowledgeable they will even be in a position to correct him where he makes a mistake because no one is a custodian of all knowledge.

For you to be successful in leadership, you must make sure that those who work with you know your stand on issues, your dos and don'ts. They must also be conversant with operational manuals and guidelines. They must also study the by-laws, or even the constitutional provisions.

When people know that you are conversant with the word or statutes and ordinances and they also see you as one who applies the rules and regulation, call it the guiding principles of leadership religiously and unbiasedly; and that you are upright in your application of all these, even an epitome of it, they will be forced, even the renegades, in their midst, to fall into place. And then you have also taught them, then they are without excuse! Another important thing a leader who desires to lead with integrity must do to succeed is being careful about the nature and quality of men and women you select to assist you in various capacities either as advisers or aids or whatever depending on your nature of leadership. I mean the men and women who are your inner caucus assistants. Depending on who they are, they are capable of making or marring your leadership.

Remember what the Bible says in 1 Cor. 15:33; it says; *Be not deceived: evil communication corrupts good manners" (KJV).* The New Living Translation (NLT) puts it this way *"Bad company corrupts good character".*

Despite your good *intentions*, there are those you bring into leadership to assist you who may end up leading you astray either through the kind of advice they give you or through other roles they play in your leadership. We have biblical examples to buttress this. It was the wrong advice from the young men to Rehoboam that caused the division of Israel into two kingdoms. When Solomon died, and Rehoboam his son took over as king, the whole of Israel came to him and said that they would be ready to support him as king on the condition that he would reduce the grievous yoke his father (Solomon) put on them. He asked them to give him three days to seek advice. He consulted the old men that worked with his father, and they advised him to speak to them politely, and to promise to treat them well. But he left them and went to the young men that grew up with him to also seek counsel. Those ones asked him to tell the people that if his father's yoke was heavy ,that the one he (Rehoboam) was bringing was going to be heavier. Hear them; *"And the young men that were grown up with him spake with him saying, thus shalt thou speak unto this people that spake unto thee saying, Thy father made our yoke heavy but make thou it lighter unto us, thus shalt thou say unto them, My little finger shall be thicker than my father's loins. And now whereas my father did lade you with a heavy yoke, I will add to your yoke; my father hath chastised you with whips, but I will chastise you with scorpions" (1 Kings. 12:10-11).*

Of course you know the rest of the story, when the people came back to him after three days and he talked to them harshly according to the counsel he received from the young men, they immediately deserted him, ten of the twelve tribes of Israel dissociated themselves from his rulership, and aligned themselves with Jeroboam, while only two tribes remained with him.

This is what an evil counsel or advice, can do. If you are an eagle, you don't flock with other bird .like turkeys or you cannot fly.

To maintain integrity in leadership, you need an understanding of what leadership actually means.

Do you see leadership as an opportunity to render service to the people? I mean do you see it as a means of righting wrongs, a means of touching lives, even as a means of bringing revival of structures, situations, individuals, groups, communities from doldrums, inactivity or even deadness to activity and liveliness? If you see leadership from this perspective, you will most assuredly do well because your focus is improvement oriented. You are not likely to listen to any counsel that runs contrary to your focus no matter from whom it comes.

On the other hand, if your understanding of leadership is as an opportunity to enrich yourself or dictate to others, then you are on your way to failure. The reason is simple, your preoccupation will be looking for loopholes in the system through which you will defraud and swindle the organization or institution. Evil- intentioned advisers will have easy access to you and you will fall prey to them. They will remind you that opportunity knocks only but once, and you should grab it fast or you lose your chance. They will remind you that nobody climbs an Iroko tree twice. I see this as an adage of fraudsters! But the truth is that if you do well in a particular position, it will be the reason for either a re-appointment or a promotion to higher positions in the present or in the near future. Goods works will always receive rewards both in the now and in the hereafter.

Beloved, we have no excuse for not leading with integrity. We must be determined to do it and to damn the consequences. We should be ready to swim against the tide, and it could occasionally be tempestuous. But rest assured, you will surely overcome, and you will be handsomely rewarded by our great Rewarder.

04

INTEGRITY IN THE WORKS OF LIFE

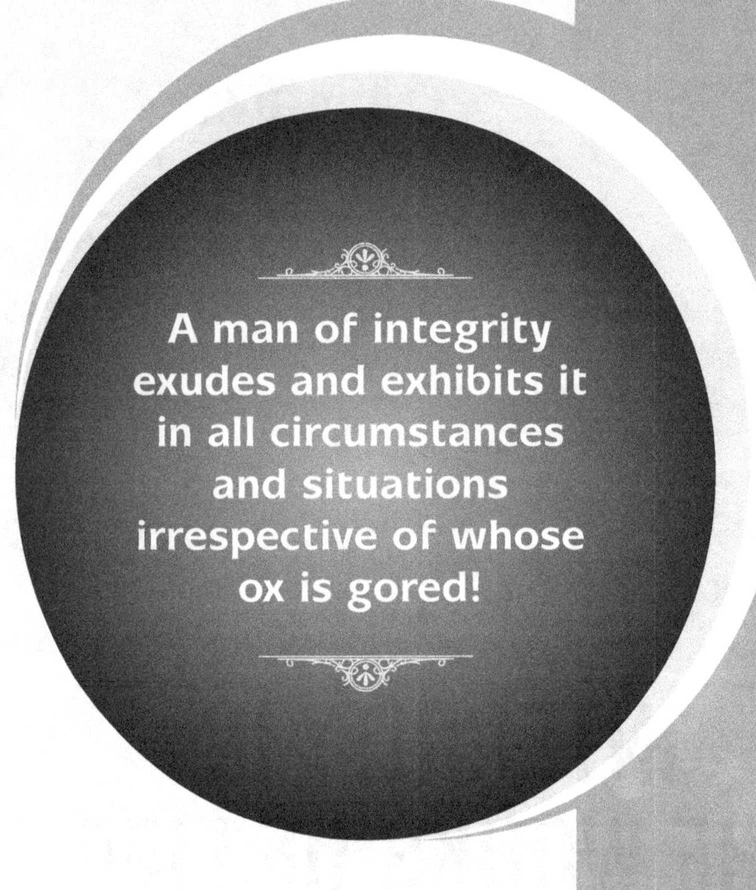
A man of integrity exudes and exhibits it in all circumstances and situations irrespective of whose ox is gored!

Four

CHAPTER FOUR

INTEGRITY IN THE WORKS OF LIFE

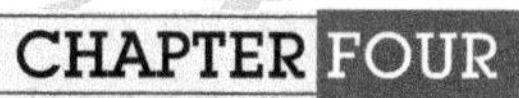

In the preceding chapter, the discussion was purely centered on integrity in leadership. It does not in any way mean that it is only leaders that are expected to show integrity in their day to day works of life. Not at all.

Rather it is because we believe that the character and characteristics of a kingdom emanate from the character of the king.

David, the Psalmist said that the precious ointment (here we can call that ointment integrity) runs down from the head unto the beard and even to the skirts of the garment (Ps. 133:2).

There is no way the head will be sick and you expect the rest of the body to be sane or well!

But for the head to be able to have the much needed peace and tranquility to perform, there must be adequate co-operation from the rest of the body.

You will also agree with me that sickness (problems) can

commence in the legs or any other part of the body, and if unchecked, it migrates to the head. So the head and all other part of the body make up the whole body, and whatever affects one member affects the others.

Note what Paul, the apostle said about the unity or the interwoven nature of different members of the body in 1 Cor. 12:25-26 *"That there should be no schism in the body; but that the members should have the same care one for another. And whether one member suffer, all the members suffer with it; or one member is honoured, all the members rejoice with it"*.

Schism means division of a group into opposing factions. If the leadership is doing everything to make sure that it is working blamelessly or in accordance with accepted principles, but in your own little corner, either as a civil/public servant, a business man, an artisan, a student or whatever, your activities are counter- productive, then you are bringing schism into the polity.

You know most of the time, it is easier for the citizenry to shout and complain that the government or the leadership is not doing well.

In the secular state or democracy, we can say we are not receiving the dividends of democracy in the form of infrastructural development, or even that we are not receiving our salaries or pensions as and when due. We conclude that the government is corrupt. But if you ask the businessman who is complaining about lack of infrastructural development when last he paid tax, it will be embarrassing to discover that he is a chronic tax evader or at best what the man pays as tax is just 10% of the actual amount he should pay. But government is supposed to use its internally generated revenue (IGR) of which tax is a major component to provide the much needed infrastructure.

Talking about taxation and taxes, granted that we as citizens especially in the states and local governments in Nigeria believe that government especially at these levels do not make judicious use of the taxes they receive, to better the lives of the masses, but rather use them to enrich themselves and their cronies, yet, we know that two wrongs have never made a right, but instead worsen the situation, therefore we do not have any good reason not to pay our taxes. We are inexcusable.

It would be a better option to pay our taxes as and when due. It will at least help us to expose their lies and corruption, and we will be in a better position to accurately criticize them.

In my country (Nigeria), 90% of the taxes paid come from civil/public servants whose taxes are deducted from the source because of the P.A.Y.E system. Without digressing from our discussion, my submission is that if we as individuals can brighten our little corners in the areas of integrity, we will all be the better for it. After all it is when numerous small individual fires come together that we get what we call a conflagration.

In our society, lack of integrity is generic in the sense that you find it in the lowest cadre of the society and the upper echelon. You find it in the messenger in the office who hides files or expects a tip for moving file or veers out for other personal matters when sent on an errand. In the same vein you find it in the CEO who asks for bribe to sign a contract or the one that siphons the company or institution's finances.

You find lack of integrity in the clerk, whether administrative or financial. You find it in both the mason or bricklayer as well as the contractor or the builder or architect.

You find absence of integrity in the hospital orderly as well as in the nurse, the pharmacist, the laboratory scientist and the medical doctor. In whatever sector of our society you look into, it is the same. In the building sector for example today we are experiencing so many buildings collapsing either while under construction, or after completion The reason is not only due to the lack of technical knowledge of the builder, but also on acts that compromise the standards. When you are supposed to use one bag of cement to mould say thirty 9-inch blocks, you, rather, as the contractor, instruct the block moulder to get fifty 9-inch blocks from just one bag of cement. Where you are expected to use 16mm iron rods, you opt for 12mm to maximize your profit. This is even when you have charged the owner by the price of 16mm rods.

What of in that situation you know quite well that what is needed for the work is say 2000 bags of cement, but you inflate it to 2500. So you now go back to either sale the extra 500 or collect the cash equivalent. Does any of the actions and many more described above show you as either a builder or contractor to be a man/woman of integrity.

Apart from your lack of integrity, do you know the level of hardship you bring to a person or institution or government when the structure you are putting up for then collapses? What of when lives are lost in that process, do you imagine the ripple effect on the society at large?

If we begin to extrapolate it, you will discover that your singular act of fraudulence has affected and afflicted many, either directly or indirectly. It is also the same way that the integrity of the righteous builder will positively affect the larger society even by enhancing the availability of infrastructure in the area of accommodation at least. Even at that, the contractor or builder still makes a profit, which is blessed by God Himself. It is the will of God that we make profit from our daily endeavours. See what the scripture tells us about making profit.

Isa. 48:17 says *"Thus saith the Lord, thy Redeemer, the Holy one of Israel; I am the LORD THY God which teacheth thee to profit, which leadeth thee by the way that thou shouldest go"*. God approves of profit. But there is a difference between profit making and profiteering. Profiteering in one sense means an unreasonable profit. An unreasonable profit is like a pyrrhic victory – a victory gotten at a great loss. You have gained because of your fraudulence or your insincerity, but the people or your clients have lost greatly! This is not of God.

Now going a little further, the Bible speaks against using

dishonest standards (or unrighteousness in judgment according to KJV) in Lev. 19:35-36.

> *"Do not use dishonest standards when measuring length, weight, or volume. Your scales and weights must be accurate. Your containers for measuring dry materials or liquids must be accurate" (NLT).*

But what we see today in our society or in the day to day business is the direct opposite of God's statutes and ordinances. Go to our petrol (or gas) stations, you will find out that 90% of the petrol pump dispensers from which we buy are grossly manipulated. I remember when I went to one of such stations to buy for my generator in the house with a container. The container was 30 litres by volume. Amazingly in this fuel station, even 34 litres of fuel dispensed from the pump could not fill a 30 litre container. This is because the fuel pump is compromised to dispense less than is approved for a given price. You can imagine the loss other buyers from such stations suffer especially as they buy directly into their vehicles tanks. And this is the norm in our society whether you are buying petrol, diesel or kerosene.

The latest practice in filling stations now are that they pump in air first into your tank. So if you came to buy say 20 litres of petrol, by the time you are leaving, you would be lucky to have gotten 16 litres.

What of cement dealers? There is what is called re-bagging. When they buy two hundred bags from the manufacturers, they re-bag them to produce two hundred and fifty bags.

So despite the fact that your bag of cement still has 50kg written on it, it is indeed about 45kg. What they have done does not reduce the price of the cement.

Go to those who sell rice in bags. Ideally a bag of rice should have about 200 cups of rice. But they also re-bag and in the end you have about 180 cups in a bag.

You see these unjust weights or measurements replicated in virtually all articles of trade in our society, whether from the big time distributors or the small time retailers. Even from some manufacturers themselves. The sizes of tablets of soap or toothpaste have all reduced over the years, but the labels remains the same.

But the one I consider as the most wicked is as it relates to pharmaceutical products. I mean the drugs human beings consume for treatment of ailments. The evil in this area is perpetrated in two ways and it affects both the quality and quantity. Today, we have our businessmen who go to China, Taiwan or India to arrange with drug companies and demand a reduction in the quality of the drugs. For example, in a tablet or capsule whose content is usually 500mg, they demand that it be reduced to about 200mg. But it will still be labeled 500mg. So ingredients that should be used for two capsules or tablets will now be used for five! This is what these heartless businessmen do.

Worse yet are those who get the empty shells or casings of these capsules, or injection powder and instead of filling them with the appropriate medical ingredients, they either fill them with powdered milk or corn flour.

Today, because of lack of integrity in business our markets and pharmacies are stockpilled with either very low quality medications or outright fake drugs that are beautifully labeled like the original – no thanks to the computer age.

Can you imagine the consequences of these evil practices to our health? People are dying in greater numbers from illnesses from which they should have survived even when the doctors have apparently made the correct diagnosis and given the correct prescriptions! Invariably, resistance to drugs is on the increase because of these low quality drugs all over our markets.

Illnesses are progressing from acute to chronic. Patients are developing complications when they should not. Recovery time from illnesses are increasing and so much man hours are lost thus slowing down an already depressed economy. All because there is lack of integrity in business.

Can you imagine the frustration and embarrassment doctors and other medical personnel face as a result of this? What of the frustration of the patients and their relations who despite the length of time it takes to recover, may also develop other complications and spend even more time and money than would ordinarily be expected in that ill health.

In a place like Nigeria where the largely poor and impoverished people find it difficult to fully pay their medical bills, some unscrupulous medical practitioners for that fear may not give the patient adequate medications both in dosage and duration of treatment. You see a doctor giving for only four days, a medication that should be taken for one week or more. Or at other times, a medication that should be taken six hourly, that is four times a day, the doctor prescribes it for eight hourly that is three times a day. This is just because the doctor's only consideration is pecuniary. But is that true to the Hippocratic oath which he swore to on the day he was sworn in as a medical doctor on his graduation. This again borders on integrity.

If we can extrapolate this a little further, we have physicians, especially surgeons who deliberately make the wrong diagnosis, because it is the one that will fetch them more money. This is worse with those who are in private practice. There have been cases where, for example, in the case of PID (Pelvic Inflammatory Disease) or salpingitis, but the doctor diagonizes it as appendicitis, just because he thinks that a surgical operation will be more financially rewarding than merely treating PID. There are even worse scenarios even where patients have been treated for cancers that they did not have! What of couples that have infertility problems? A lot of them cannot open their mouths to tell you what they have passed through in the hands of some doctors who have milked them dry and left them more frustrated than they were when they came to them initially.

That is why the current baby miracle fertility is taking place somewhere in a popular town in a South South State of Nigeria. Every woman that goes there even if they are post-menopausal for more than ten years comes back with babies they claim they delivered by themselves. What goes on there is a mystery nobody has ever bordered to unravel.

But time will tell the authenticity of those claims, whether they are spurious or true!

Shifting focus a little from the medics, let us also consider the way some laboratory scientists or technologists practice their profession. Early in my years of full-time private medical practice, when I had not yet set up a medical laboratory, I employed a young lab technologist whose duty was to collect the patients sample, do the simple tests our little lab could afford and then take the others to a designated bigger laboratory where they could be done. That young man claimed to be a christian in the true sense of the word. So I trusted him, but he began to culture all sorts of micro-organisms, both "culturable" and non-culturable. So I began to investigate him, and in the process I found out that in a number of cases he would take the patient specimens, but he would not go to the lab, but would stay in his house and give a result/report from the tentative diagnosis I had made! He would just use the money the patient paid for the laboratory investigation, but stays in his house and "cooks up" a report. What a terrible act! Of course that ended my association with him.

Such acts among so many others are still happening today. Reports and results are still written from the head, not from the laboratory investigations. The matter has even gone out of hand since 99% of laboratories (the privately owned) have diversified their practices. They now pose as doctors. In fact not only pose, but bear that title with impunity. I know of one in the town I live who has also gone ahead to put some hospital beds where patients are admitted. Their common slogan is "The man who discovers the illness is also the best person that should treat it"! Incredible! To this group of people, the process of diagnosis only involves taking a specimen to the laboratory! So the major issue of clerking the patient which involves history taking and physical examinations to elicit signs and symptoms are no longer necessary! What would you call this? An asinine and fiendish judgment or what? But this all borders on not being contented and proud of your position and profession just because you want to make more money for yourself. You do not care what the consequences of this would be. Would you say that such persons in such professions have integrity?

The nagging question is; does it mean that one cannot achieve goals in life, whether goals of becoming materially wealthy or becoming prominent, without being dubious or dishonest?

A final word for the medics is to inform us that when you begin to write all sorts of letters for people who want to circumvent their court cases by telling the court that they are sick, when it is indeed a lie very well known to you. Just because you want to be paid a fee, you ridicule the nobility of your profession. Even when you are giving out sick certificates to undeserving people to cover their dereliction of duty, or unnecessary exemptions of duty for non-existing health situations, just for purely pecuniary considerations, your integrity is very questionable. A man of integrity exudes and exhibits it in all circumstances and situations irrespective of whose ox is gored!

Some years ago, a particular minister of the federal capital territory (FCT) Abuja began to pull down so many buildings that contravened Abuja master plan. And even the high and mighty were affected. People had managed to fraudulently obtain these lands even in areas reserved either for drainage or sewage or for recreations or even for future roads and streets and built in those areas. FCT urban planning/development authority approved all those buildings and they began to build despite the fact that it was contrary to the master plan. They just collected money from these ones and gave approvals. Thank God for that minister.

But this is what is replicated in almost all the cities in Nigeria. And one of the immediate consequences is increase in flooding because the water ways created ab initio in the master plans have all been blocked by buildings and all forms of structures.

Some town planners in Nigeria are people of little or no integrity. I mean majority of them. Any type of structure can be sited anywhere. I have seen cooking gas refilling stations existing in between residential houses. So is the allocation of places of worship, be it a church or mosque in big cities. Many buildings are so close to major high ways, and this has caused disaster several times. Some heavy duty vehicles and all sorts of vehicles run into peoples houses when they lose control or their brakes fell, thus causing fatalities. Builders do not observe the approved distance structures are by law expected to be from the roads. This has also made road expansions very difficult in many cities because trying to expand the road or street would lead to demolition of so many buildings.

The irony is that when these buildings are under construction, the town planning authority would come and write; "STOP WORK OR ILLEGAL STRUCTURE – DEMOLISH BY UCDA" or whatever name they go by depending on whether it is a capital development authority (CDA) or town planning authority (TPA) or local government development authority (LGDA).

In most instances, work on the site is halted for a short period and only resumed when they have bribed the authority that wrote that. But in some other instances, work is not halted at all, either because the owner of the structure is a "big shot" in society or in government. He therefore only needs to call those concerned on phone and find out what they wanted. He settles them and work continues. You rarely ever see a building demolished, and it would probably be because the owner of the structure either refused to "play ball", didn't give enough bribe, or it was a politically motivated action.

This lack of integrity of the town planning authorities has made our towns look chaotic. Construction of roads have been so badly impeded. In the town where I reside, the World Bank Housing Estate is like a slum or ghetto because houses were never built to specifications. And other slums are also fast developing, no thanks to the nefarious activities of the town planners and their cohorts.

When you are in an aircraft, you will notice the difference

in the planning of most foreign cities as the aircraft is landing as against the chaotic and planlessness of Nigerian cities, except Abuja. The difference is always as clear as crystal and in fact brings shame and ridicule to our country. This is even when you compare it with poorer African countries. This is what lack of integrity in the place of work does to a country. Even the few cities that our colonial masters planned very well and created recreational facilities and parks, even zoological gardens have all been defaced badly. Houses have been built in those facilities because when the military and civilian governments came, being people who never cared about beauty and aesthetics, they quickly allocated such places to themselves and their cronies in dubious transactions and built their towers, hotels, gas stations, and all that are in such places. Today, many of those cities lack gardens, parks or any such places we can take our children to for recreation.

In the state capital where I live, no such thing like recreational facility exists anywhere, even when it is supposed to be a modern capital, it has been turned into a slum by the selfish and insatiable aggrandizement or acquisition of land and property by past and present governments.

Even the place that used to be a cattle market that a former military government removed, and was skeletally turned into a park, and everyone was waiting for a government that would come and develop the park well. But, alas because of our political leaders unquenchable greed for acquisition of land and property, they took it over and turned it into a shopping mall!

The irony is that these same people take their families from Nigeria to Orlando Florida in United States to visit the Disney Wonder land. They go to Singapore to visit Singapore Sintosa park or flower and insect gardens, at a great financial cost to the state or nation!

Who says that the judgment of God will not be visited upon such people. See what the scriptures say in Galatian 6:7, *"Be not deceived, God is not mocked for whatsoever a man soweth, that shall he also reap".*

The planlessness and the chaotic nature of our towns reminds me of JP Clark's poem titled "IBADAN", which I read as a literature student in secondary school. It reads

Ibadan

Running splash of rust

And gold-flung and scattered

Among seven hills like broken

China in the sun

What touches my fancy there is the phrase "gold-flung and scattered" and "like broken china in the sun". Even though Ibadan is one of the largest cities in Africa, yet the "scattered" there depicts the planlessness that is why it has been difficult for subsequent governments to have good success in giving Ibadan the good face-lift it requires.

Some roads end nowhere, some start very wide and end very narrow because of the poor and reckless arrangement ofbuildings.

But what we see in Ibadan will become a tip of the iceberg to what will happen in the town I live and some other towns in my country in the years to come if nothing is done about the way town planners, urban development authorities and government agents are recklessly approving the sighting of all forms of buildings, whether residential, commercial or other utility buildings. It is common sight to see a filling station standing next to a residential building or a church building standing next to a residential building. No designated areas.

All these are as a result of fraudulent approvals of building plans. You can build whatever you want wherever you choose as long as you can bribe enough the authorities concerned or you have somebody who is powerful in government.

Nobody thinks about the implications of these wrongly located buildings. Already flood has started sacking some homes. What do we say about buildings that are located less than two meters from major highways. They were all approved by designated or recognized authorities, who were more pecuniary minded than anything else. But the question is; does there reckless and fraudulent approvals as well as crass disregard for the rule of law represent integrity? You now understand the extent to which lack of integrity can affect every aspect of our lives. But this is what you see at every levels of our civil or public service from the permanent secretary or director general to the messenger in the office. The decadence is overwhelming and dumbfounding!

This has seriously paralyzed and stiffed activity. Let me give you three small examples of what happens in the ministry. Some years ago, the water tanker that supplied water to an institute that was concerned with agriculture broke down. And going through the usual protocol or bureaucratic system, those concerned were asked to evaluate the problem with the tanker and bring a quotation of what would be needed to repair it. At the end of the day, they brought a highly padded quotation of about N99,000.00 (ninety-nine thousand naira}. So the head of department said, there was no money to do that repair then. That, of course, was in the days when the naira still had a great value. For that reason, the water tanker was parked for six to nine months. One day, one of the researchers who desperately needed to use the water tanker asked for permission of the HOD to go repair the tanker himself so he can use it for his project and it was granted. He called in an auto mechanic, who evaluated all that is needed to be done, and gave a bill of thirteen thousand naira (N13,000.00). He repaired it completely, and still made his gain!

In another development, at a particular ministry of utilities, after a particular day of heavy rain storm, a big tree located close a building in the ministry felled and a branch hit the building slightly and damaged the roof minimally. This was early in the 90's.

Then the ministry requested tenders to effect the repair of the damaged roof. A friend put in a tender of about N18,000,00 naira, the HOD said no, that the quotation was too small. Later on he gave it to somebody else who quoted N60,000.00.

A colleague of mine narrated a story of what happened in his place of work – a government owned hospital. A clergy friend of his brought in some equipment from abroad which he believed his hospital would need. He persuaded the minister who willingly donated the physiotherapy equipment free of charge to his hospital.

But there was also another equipment, which was certified to be very good, and fully functional, he asked the hospital to pay him a paltry sum of N1.5million even though the market value then was about N3.0million. He needed the money to fund the scholarship he had given to some indigent students. But the hospital board of directors met and said that if they paid him straight N1.5 million, they would gain nothing out of it for themselves; so they said the only way they could buy it was if the reverend gentleman agreed to a cost of N5.0million in paper, though they would still give him his N1.5 million, and share the balance among themselves. The man refused because he told them he was a man of God with integrity and could not do that. So the board refused to approve the purchase of that very needed equipment for their surgical theatre. And when he visited the country again, he came and carried away the equipment after it had stayed there for more than six months.

Immediately, another hospital in the Northern part of the country that heard of it bought it at N2.0million! My friend was heartbroken because he desperately needed it in his department to enhance his practice and the safety of his patients. They had none of this vital machine as at that time!

But for what reason is a board of directors established or created in an institution? Is it not to enhance the overall welfare of that institution? That is on paper. But in reality, most boards of director are scavengers, or even looters. Largely board appointments are seen as political settlements for loyal party members. It's given to them as their gold mines.

They only come to enhance or fill their pockets. They create a serious financial pressure on the institution. They lodge in the choicest hotels, eat expensively, sometimes with their ladies (not necessarily their wives). And even if the meeting is for three days, they can lodge for upward of one week before and after the meeting and they expect the institution to pick up the bills. And when they are leaving, they do so with fat sitting allowances, plus other privileges they receive at different times and occasions in the year. You must employ their children, girlfriends, relatives and acquaintances whether there is space or not. In fact, a lot of institutions have gone bankrupt or completely closed down because of the activities of members of board of directors. That was one of the major causes of the death of the only brewing industry in my town of residence. And for more than ten years it was closed down before it was recently resuscitated by private investors. Most CEOs,

MDs, GMs do better when there are no Boards of Directors. You see some of them trying to do some laudable things within the interregnum of two boards.

All these and many more depict the dearth of integrity that is synonymous with every facet of our being in our nations and continent despite what we may proclaim or even appear to represent.

This is exactly why when anybody is given any appointment, even as a member of the board of directors in a tertiary institution or of even a hospital, on the day of their inauguration, he goes with his people carrying musical instruments – everybody dancing and celebrating. They celebrate in pump and pageantry! Why? He has just been appointed a member of a board, but not just that, he has arrived, his time to steal has come. It is time to loot. God help us.

And in order to meet up to the expectations of his people, he has to do all sorts of orthodox and unorthodox things. He has to play all sorts of crooked games, do all forms of unlawful things to make it! Even when he is reluctant to do it, his people will rebuke him, ill-advise him or even reprimand him.

I don't want to attempt to go into the situation in our civil and public services. I may never exhaust what needs to be discussed because the level of decadence or rot is overwhelming. It stinks and it has sunk to its lowest ebb. It got worse during the military era when all sorts of nomenclature were introduced into the system to suit their retrogressive purposes. Then it worsened with the advent of politician who completely politicized the public service and all forms of political settlements, tribalism and nepotism being introduced into it. Somebody comes in as a special adviser or assistant to a governor, he had not been in the civil service ab initio. His was purely a political appointment. But suddenly, he transits from special adviser after four years to a director general or even a permanent secretary! That way, he begins to head the core civil servants who have served many years and who actually understand the system. And having been so favoured, he becomes an agent or tool in the hands of the political leader to commit all forms of malfeasance. That way the system is polluted. Things that used to be sacred have become desecrated. Other officers follow suit, especially those who work under him. Promotion no longer comes by merit, but only if you are a praise-singer or a mole to the powers that be. And if you try to protest against what is going on, you will either be transferred or even retired. And because people do not want to lose their jobs, they queue behind that powers that be. That is why there is an adage that has gained prominence in our political system. It says, "that the goats will always follow the man that has the palm fronds". What a mess we have found ourselves in. What is now practiced in the civil service is called the philosophy of the jungle, or the "dog eat dog" philosophy. At this juncture, let me remind us of what scripture say in the following verses of the Bible.

In Rom. 2:1,Apostle Paul declares *"Therefore thou art inexcusable, O man…."* That is you cannot say that your reason for being part of the rot, that is, being an active participant in the rot is because the system forced you, because the same Bible says in Exodus 23:2 that *"Thou shall not follow a multitude to do evil,"*. Also Prov. 24:10 say *"If thou faint in the day of adversity, thy strength is small"*.

The story of the three Hebrew slaves or captives-Shadrach, Meshach and Aded-nego-who refused to worship the molten image made by Nebuchadnezzar, the powerful Babylonian king even at the point of death when they were thrown into the fiery furnace that was heated seven times over, but for the intervention of God himself (see Dan 3). Even Daniel himself also refused to worship a mere man, the king Darius, as god even for a period of 30 days. He also was thrown into the den of the lions. Again God intervened. (See Dan. chapter 6).

Yet there are men who have paid with their lives resisting the rot in the system. A man like John Hus (1372-1415), a catholic priest and reformer who resisted the terrible rot in the Catholic church even until that day on 6th July 1415 when he was stripped, tied to the stake naked and burnt alive by the order of the catholic authorities. Even on the stake, at the last minute Hus refused to recant his belief in the truth of the gospel of Jesus Christ, which he preached elaborately and openly despite all threats. But today all those truths of the scripture which he preached have virtually been accepted by the Catholic Church. On December 17, 1999, Pope John Paul II told an international symposium: "Today on the eve of the great Jubilee, I feel the need to express regret for the cruel death inflicted on

John Hus". But the Pope's announcement took 584 years to come. This is by the way.

All I am saying is that except we make up our minds, especially those of us who confess to be believers in Christ Jesus, to tow the part of integrity in our works of life, the system will continue to get worse even for generations to come. It makes the heart to bleed when you observe that even believers are part and parcel of the rot or decadence whether in the market place, civil service, judiciary, health, education, anywhere, mention it. Even those who are ministers of the gospel! May I once again remind us that the Bible says that "we are the light of the world Matt.5:14-16 Says, *"Ye are the light of the world. A city that is set on an hill cannot be hid. Neither do men light a candle and put it under a bushel, but on a candle stick and it giveth light unto all that are in the house. Let your light so shine before men, that they may see your good works and glorify your father which is in heaven"*. Our light can only shine when we show honesty transparency, faithfulness, and diligence in all our works of life.

05

THE ROT IN OUR EDUCATIONAL SYSTEM

As the corruption in our country has gotten worse with successive governments, so has the corruption in every facet of our society got worse with that of the educational section being probably one of the most affected and afflicted.

Five

CHAPTER FIVE

THE ROT IN OUR EDUCATIONAL SYSTEM

As a young boy in primary school in the 1970s, I so valued education that nothing else mattered to me. Like believers of the early days sang "Take the whole world, and give me Jesus" showing their passion for Christ and for making heaven, the song (in my heart) was "take the whole world and give me education", also showing my passion for education! I also had a passion for becoming a medical doctor, and nothing else. So I used every strength I could muster to bulldoze whatever would appear like an obstacle on my way to becoming a medical doctor, as mathematics wanted to be. I conquered it. I had also always boasted that my brain was a step up transformer. So I could always step it up to do whatever or achieve whatever I wanted to do or achieve. But now I know better, that it is not of him that wills nor of him that runs, but of God that shows mercy (Rm 9:16). And that every wisdom comes from God Himself (James 1:5).

Also whenever I saw any person that has a Ph.D, I almost felt like worshipping him. What is more when that person is a professor in any discipline! In fact this was one of the things that motivated me and propelled me to receive Jesus Christ as my Lord and savior on that fateful day of 16th May 1987 at a Full Gospel Business Men's Fellowship International Breakfast meeting at Ile-Ife. I had attended this breakfast meeting just to enjoy their free breakfast that fateful morning. It was not my first, because I also attended that of the previous month April 1987. But I left after the meal function. However on this fateful 16th May 1987 morning, I came as usual to eat free food. One of those who were lined up to give the testimony of their encounters with Christ was the then Vice Chancellor of University of Ibadan, the premier university in Nigeria. Of course the man was a Ph.D holder and a professor. When the man was introduced and he started sharing the story of how he encountered Christ, I was startled and rattled. I was only a final year medical student in the medical school who was waiting to sit for the only re -sit exam I had had all through my medical school education. A re-sit exam in surgery only, that was politicized and for which I spent 15 extra months in the medical school; note, not repeating a class. That is a story for another day. But you understand my melancholic state then. And before then I had always believed that those who got born again were the lowly, frustrated and poverty stricken class. But here was a Ph.D holder, a professor and a Vice Chancellor giving a testimony of his becoming born again. And this man was in the class of men I almost worshipped as God. I just did not see how again I could resist receiving Jesus in my life. When the altar call was made, I promptly ran to the front and surrendered my life to my Maker. And life has never been the same again since then. That was the level of the influence of education in my life. But that was indeed the days when a Ph.D degree was a reflection of great academic excellence by the holder. And becoming a professor was also a great scholarly attainment not a political award. Men and women who had PhDs or were university professors could stand their kind anywhere in the world. But is it the same today?

When I was in the primary school in 1970, I used to write letters and land agreements for illiterate relations and neighbours in my village who either desired to communicate with their children or relations in the urban centres through letters or who had land deals, either outright buying of the land or leasing it. I did that as a primary school pupil. Writing application letters was a very easy thing to do in those days. But today you dare not ask even a school certificate holder to do that. Especially if they attended public schools. We have had terrible experiences with primary and secondary school students we had brought to stay with us in my house over the years. Some of them in primary six could not even spell their names correctly, what more reading or writing the simplest words. We have had to start them afresh. Our most current experience with this issue was extremely disheartening. He was twelve years old when he came to us from his village. Actually his father was admitted in the government hospital where I work following his involvement in a ghastly motor accident. He was in his farm when a vehicle ran off the road and came and hit him badly in the farm. He was in coma for a long time and his wife had to take all the children to the hospital to sleep in corridors and open places. We decided to take one of them to live with us to ameliorate their sufferings. He was supposed to be in primary five, but he could not even spell his name. He could not spell "is" nor could he pronounce it. What would have been best for him was to enrol him in primary one or even the nursery. But how can you do that to a twelve year old! So we enrolled him in primary three in a private school. It was a battle. It took more than one year before there was a flicker of light in the tunnel. But he was salvaged eventually at least to a manageable level. He may not become tomorrow's medical doctor or engineer, but he will become somebody. The damage had already been done. On the contrary my mother who I understand only stopped her education at primary three or so before she married, reads very well and even writes well.

Now to buttress the terrible rot in our educational system and the horribly fallen standard of education, let me tell you a few stories.

I run a private clinic as part time. Sometime ago, a young girl who had trained elsewhere came to be employed as an auxillary nurse in my clinic. During the interview, I noticed that she had A1 in mathematics, with some other wonderful results. Then I asked her what was her business becoming an auxiliary nurse with that kind of result. I enquired to ascertain if that result truly belonged to her. She insisted it was hers. But she said she had nobody to train her. I had pity on her and employed her. However, I discovered over time that whenever it was her turn to prepare the account and present to me, there was always terrible errors in addition and in writing the amount of money in figures. She could write one thousand one hundred as 1000100 or 100100 and not 1100. Now this was somebody who claimed to have scored an A1 in mathematics. What really happened? How on earth did she score A1 in maths? Your guess is as good as mine. We shall come back to this later. There was also another young girl with an impressive secondary school certificate, so to say, whose father secured a job for with a local government. On the day she went to collect her letter of employment, the officer in charge gave her a copy of the employment letter and asked her to write "ORIGINAL COPY COLLECTED BY ME", and then sign. He dictated it for her and left. Fifteen minutes later, when he returned the young girl was still there trying to write it. He dictated it again in case she did not get it the first time. For where! She could not write it. He now wrote it on a piece of paper, and asked her to copy it. By now she was sweating profusely. She could not copy it. He now told her that if she could not write this simple statement, and could not even copy it, then there is no way you can do the job. She lost the job and the person who brought her took her away in shame. How did she get the certificate? Before I tell you the other stories, let me inform you that after my West African School Certificate in 1976, in which I passed out with grade 1, I got an appointment as an auxiliary teacher in 1977 to teach in a secondary school – St Catherine Secondary School Mbieri – Imo State. When I got there, they had no biology teacher for classes four and five. So as a school cert holder and a teenager yet, I taught biology in class five and prepared them for school certificate examination and they did well. I also taught integrated science in class 1. How many school certificate holders can do that today?

In another instance, there was this young lady who had completed her NYSC. Her mother (a widow) was our family friend and we had known her since she was in the primary school. She said she wanted me to be one of her referees in the application she was writing to do a clinical nutrition and Dietetics in a teaching hospital. Of course I consented and she brought the application she wrote for me to see. Behold it was full of errors, so many mistakes, omissions, wrong spellings. In short it did not have the nature or format of an application. I told her things to re-write, spelling to correct and the format to use. She thanked me profusely and left. But when she brought back the corrected copy days later, there was not much, if any improvement at all. So I now had to scribble something in between the lines in the application to help her make a proper correction. Yet when she came back after a few days, there were still very obvious deficiencies. I had no choice but to take another sheet of paper and I rewrote the whole application, and asked her to go and type and bring it back for me to see. That was how that issue of writing application was settled. I mean, a university graduate.

Now to my fourth story to further buttress the high level of decadence in our educational system. I didn't witness this personally, but somebody whom I can trust his testimony did.

A young lady, the daughter of a highly placed bank chief executive, graduated with a second class upper division in

Banking and Finance from a Nigerian university. After her National Youth Service Corp (NYSC), her father appealed to another highly placed chief executive in another bank in another town to give his daughter employment in his bank. The man readily obliged and asked him to send the daughter over to him.

When she arrived, he placed her in a well air-conditioned office and told her that there is already a job for her. But he explained to her that she had to write a formal application that has to be documented. Therefore he gave her a sheet of paper to write the application. He left for other things. He came back after about an hour to take the application. The lady had messed up the paper and was sweating profusely. The man asked what the matter was, she said she needed another paper as there were several cancellations in the first paper. He obliged her, and this time around gave her sheets of paper. But he sensed what was wrong. However, he kept quiet and went away. He gave her more time, yet when he came back after a long time, the lady was now sweating more profusely in a chilling air-conditioned room. She had not yet succeeded in writing an application for the job. This bank chief executive, went out and called her father on phone and told him what had happened. He told her father that if he continued to ask his daughter to write this application, she might have a heart attack or cardiac arrest. Her father retorted "Send that fool back to me". She is a disgrace, I know that she couldn't have made that degree by herself!

That was how also this job or employment was aborted.

I have decided to tell these stories to give you a glimpse of the present state of our educational system. Interview the teachers themselves, and the outlook will be gloomier.

But why would it not be so? The system has become extremely corrupted. And if something drastic is not done, it will still get worse.

Right from 1977 (remember Expo '77) which was the advent of the leakage of West African Examination Council (WAEC) papers for West African School Certificate Exams (WASCE) till today, the matter has gone from bad to worse. Despite the stringent measures taken then to mitigate it, including sending some of the culprits to jail, the matter has never abated. In fact what happened then is a child's play to what is happening now. Cheating in examination has become institutionalized. As the corruption in our country has gotten worse with successive governments, so has the corruption in every facet of our society got worse with that of the educational section being probably one of the most affected. and afflicted. It has now affected every level of our education right from the kindergarten to the post graduate and the professional level.

As more emphasis is being laid on paper qualification above every other criteria for employment, admission and political office aspirations, so has the quest for certificate possession at all levels increased either by hook or crook.

This has even been made worse by the frequent strike actions undertaken by teachers from the primary to the university level to press home their legitimate demands from corrupt governments that are not performing. Sometimes these strikes are for them to be paid their basic salaries and allowances. Today you see teachers in so many states not getting their salaries for upward of six to twelve months or even more. And except they go on strike, governments cannot fulfill their agreements during negotiations. So schools can be closed down for upward of 3-6 months in an academic year, and government does not give a damn. However, when they manage to resume, they condense what should be taught in three months to one month and then take exams. This way students learn little or nothing. This has drastically reduced the standard of education in the country. And this continues in every academic session. This is the bane of the public schools and universities in Nigeria. This has made the teachers turn themselves into traders or business men and women. Some take their wares to school, and spend more time selling them from class to class, than in teaching. Others spend part of their time in school and part in their shops even during school hours. Would you blame them? They no longer know when their salary will be paid. It could be once in three to four months. So diligence is completely lost.

I remember in those days in the 1980's and late 1970's when my father was still teaching. Salaries were not regular, and was paid in percentages, courtesy of what they called "IKE FORMULA" after the name of the military governor of the then Imo State, IKE NWACHUKWU. My father used to ride a Honda Benley Motorcycle. Because he had to pay our school fees and also feed us, what he did was to partly use his motorcycle for transporting passengers early in the morning before going to school and during recreation time and after school hours. All in his bid to make ends meet.

Other measures that teachers took to make ends meet was that in the primary schools, they monetized handwork. Pupils no longer brought brooms, baskets and all that as handwork, they now had to pay it in cash. That was how arts and craft was killed in the primary school. In our days, we all made brooms, baskets, etc, from palm fronds. These we used as handwork in school, and indeed made some at home and sold in the local markets to make money to help our parents and ourselves. All that is history now. No more "handwork" it is now "MONEY WORK". These were the little ways decadence began to creep into our educational system. Who should we blame? The teacher that keeps struggling to make ends meet for his family. Or the government that abdicated its responsibility of paying the teacher their salaries. The Bible says in 1 Tim 5:18, *"For the scripture saith, thou shalt not muzzle the ox that treadeth out the corn. And, the labouer is worthy of his reward" see also 1 Cor. 9:9. Also Jere. 22:13 says; "woe unto him that buildeth his house by unrighteousness, and his chambers by wrong; that useth his neigbour's service without wages, and giveth him not for his work"*.

It is important that those in authority understand that it is sinful to fail to pay workers (including the teachers) their salaries. There is also a WOE that follows non-payment of the wages of the labourer.

Furthermore, for possibly this same reason of not being paid their salaries, and as a survival strategy that eventually dove-tailed into greed, the teachers at the secondary and tertiary levels have also monetized their marks or scores in their subjects and courses. I will return to this later.

Now there is a serious erosion of integrity and honesty in the educational system. Both the parents, the teachers, the invigilators as well as WAEC and NECO officials are all aiding and abetting this evil.

There are now special miracle centres for WAEC and NECO exams all over the country. WAEC and NECO officials know about these centres. What makes these centres special is that in these places there is a free for all exam malpractice. You copy as you like, you can bring in somebody else to take the exam for you. And for each subject, there are people (teachers and undergraduates) in an adjacent room solving the questions and sending them inside. Both the teachers and invigilators look the other way because they have been heavily paid or settled! So students now leave their schools and go and enroll in those centers for exams. Their parents pay for them to take the exams in such places. It is like an open book exam. That was how possibly my auxiliary nurse made her A1 in Mathematics. What matters here is for you to get the good grades, it does not matter how you did it or if you can ever defend it.

This same system takes place even in the schools. I remember the experience my friend Collins, a true child of God who is now in Canada had in a secondary school. He was hired to teach Chemistry in a girls' school some years ago. He was employed in the second term of that academic year. They didn't have a Chemistry teacher in their first term and these were final year (exams) students. So he diligently taught them during school hours and conducted evening lessons to meet up the foregone lessons. The authorities of this supposedly Christian school owned by one of the main line denomination told Collins that on the exam day (WASCE), he would be needed to sit in the staff or any other designated room and be solving the Chemistry question which will then be taken into the exam hall to the students. He was assured that the invigilators had been paid, even the police men had been taken care of. So nothing to worry about! He bluntly refused, and told them that as a true believer in Christ, he will not be involved in such exam malpractice. He bluntly refused to do it, and at the end of that exam, they terminated his appointment.

The story I have just told is what happens in more than 70% of our secondary schools, whether public or private, whether Christian or not! Only a very few we know of, especially the private, truly Christian schools refuse to do so. Majority are neck deep into it. The teachers and the school authorities connive with invigilators and security officials to achieve this. So most of the time these days when you hear that this or that school is doing very well in either WAEC or NECO exams, don't be carried away. Try to investigate it first. Find out what they do with those extra monies the students pay outside the normal exam registration fees.

These students, knowing that both their parents and their teachers (a lot of whom are the product of the same cheating system) are willing to pay the extra fees and cooperate are no longer willing to burn the midnight candle to prepare for the exams. After all their parents will pay. The teachers will co-operate and the invigilators will not mind because after the exams they will smile to the banks. So students spend the time in playing internet games with phones, sleeping, eating and getting involved in other extra-curricular activities, instead of studying. Yes, dear invigilators and teachers, you may smile to the bank with money, but it is likened to bread of deceit, and a wealth not rightly made. Hear what the Bible says about that in Prov. 20:17; Bread of deceit is sweet to a man; but afterwards his mouth shall be filled with gravel". Also in Jeremiah. 17:11 "As the partridge sitteth on eggs, and hatcheth them not; so he that getteth riches, and not by right, shall leave them in the midst of his days and at the end shall be a fool" (KJV).

Today, many private schools use such false results from WAEC and NECO to woo parents to bring their children and wards to these schools. But some innocent and naïve parents, who think that all that glitters is gold send their children and wards to such schools. We must be careful and prayerful before we choose schools for our wards

These deceits and falsehood are the things you see in a society that suffers from a dearth of integrity; a society in which anything goes; a society where the end justifies the means; a society where evil,fraud and dishonesty are celebrated; a society that is so parochial in its thinking and a society that operates on the philosophy of the fowl: "eat, eat today for there is no tomorrow". Those who aid and abate these evil practices in our educational system either for selfish or pecuniary reasons either do not realized or do not care to realize the debilitating injury with which they afflict the system. Or to put it more succinctly, the evil legacy they are bequeathing to the future generation.

All right, let's go a little further so you may have a better understanding. The primary school pupils of today are the secondary school students of tomorrow. The secondary school students of today are the university students of tomorrow, and the undergraduates of today are the graduates of tomorrow. They are also the post-graduate students of tomorrow and ultimately, the professors, doctors, lawyers, engineers, economists, teachers, technocrats and even the political leaders of tomorrow.

Now when these students have from the primary school levels been introduced to examination malpractice, it becomes difficult at a later stage to convince them that there is, indeed, an honest and correct way of doing things. What is more when they have the open support of their parents.

In our days, we took entrance exams into secondary schools, and people could miss going to secondary school for one or two years because they had not passed such exams. I remember in 1970 I came first in one of such entrance exams in my local government. And in those days when there were no telephones, but poor postal services, the principal of that school – PATER NONSTER SECONDARY SCHOOL, EKWEREAZU, MBAISE, sent two men on a bicycle to trace my village and bring my result to our home. But despite all that, my father had a better choice, and I obeyed him. Today, though entrance exams still take place, but whether your child passes, or not, he assuredly gets a school. What more with so many private schools, looking for students. The same thing has afflicted our tertiary education. Even if you cannot pass the JAMB, UTME, there are many private universities that will admit you. The most important question is, do you have the money to pay? Gradually, all those factors that would make a student or pupil to study hard are being eroded. For example, also in our days WASCE results were graded, depending on the aggregate you scored, on the best six subjects, which must include English language and Mathematics passed with at least credit (C) score. So you could have grade one with distinction, grade 1, grade 2, grade 3, and later they added SR.(?Sorry Repeat)

How well individual schools performed, or their positions in each years school certificate exams was determined by the number of students that passed in grade one. So then if you passed out in grade one and above, everyone knows that you are a hot brain and of course passing entrance into a higher institution to study the major professional courses was almost assured. But if you had grade 3 or SR, it is obvious that you must have to repeat, or that though you had a good aggregate, but that you did not pass either mathematics or English or both.

But today, it has been watered down, the grades have been abolished. A student now comes after results are released to tell you, they gave me four subjects or five as the case may be, as if they (WAEC) decide by merely looking at your face how many subjects you will be awarded. Some of those subjects were all scores “P7 or P 8” - the poorest passes.

And because those gradations ;1,2 3, that portrays the level of intelligence or diligence a student has put into studying are no more there, enthusiasm and drive are all gone!

But more importantly, today as I have already stated, many students who brandish high scores in school certificate exams or NECO, are not brandishing the products of their brains, but those of all forms of examination malpractice. That was why my auxiliary nurse with A1 in mathematics could not correctly write numericals. That was why the other one could not write “original copy collected by one”.

These same students will find their ways into the universities and other tertiary institutions by hook or crook. There in the university, they will continue with their fraudulent systems which they now see as the only way forward. And they will perfect at this level.

You see, the rot is like a cankerworm. It is hydra-headed. Today people get admissions into the universities even when they did not pass the UTME (Unified Tertiary Matriculation Examinations). And indeed in some universities, if you can pay the amount of money required as a substitute for passing the exam,(amount ranging from five hundred thousand to one million naira), you will surely get admitted into whatever course of study you desire, including medicine, law and engineering. It has become a veritable means for vice chancellors, registrars and other highly placed university officers to make money.

Sometimes, the admissions meant for those who passed and have no body to speak for them will be sold to the children of the high and mighty; the politician, the rich, and all that. But in those days when there was still some levels of integrity and transparency in the system, it was not so. I remember some university dons that had their appointments terminated because they tried to influence the admission of their wards or children into some choice courses contrary to standing policies. Who will ever do that today. There is indeed a dearth and death of integrity.

Those who got admitted without meriting it and who also got their WASC or NECO results from special centres when they came in will surely have another system devised for them to pass "successfully" through the universities with their degrees.

This is why examination malpractice is very rampant in higher institutions. Some copy things into the exam halls. And they hide what they have copied in terrible and sacred or supposedly sacred parts of the body where invigilators will not dare check or else they will be accused of sexual harassment. Some even copy on the skin of their thighs and other parts of the body as if they are tattooing. Even married women and fathers do what I am telling you, including the clergy.

A friend of mine who went to do a post graduate dploma in education in one of the universities, though an engineer, because he is a school proprietor, told a story of how a woman who wears the clerical collar to school and to exam hall copies shamelessly. Yet when they come into the exam hall, she will be the one to call for them to pray before the exam. When my friend confronted her about this double standard, she did not deny it, but said that, that is the more reason why they should pray, so that God will forgive the past "copying" (and probably secure the current ones). This tells you the level to which peoples consciences have been seared with hot iron. Apostle Paul explains in 1 Tim. 4:1-2 that "Now the spirit speaketh expressly, that in the latter times some shall depart from the faith, giving heed to reducing spirits, and doctrines of devils, speaking lies in hypocrisy, having their conscience seared with a hot iron".

There is also the leakage of the exam question either by the lecturers themselves to their mistresses on grounds of their immoral relationships or to the highest bidders, be they male or female students. Sometimes also the leakage is not from the lecturers, but from those whose duty it is to process and print them. That's one of the reasons some schools introduced multiple choice questions (MCQ). Then you also have this thing they now call "SORTING". This usually happens after the exams when a student notices that his/her performance was poor during the exam. Or seeing that the marks they scored were very low in a course, or they had outright failure, they can go to the lecturer. Most times , these are those gullible and dirty lecturers, who also passed through the same sorting or similar methods, so they negotiate with them at a price the type of grade they want in that course ranging from A to C. Some, especially the ladies, negotiate with their bodies. These are some of the ways people obtain their degrees by cashing in on both the moral laxity and the quest for wealth of the authorities.

This decadence in our education system in the tertiary institutions has not only affected the undergraduate studies. It has also afflicted the graduate studies. Today a lot of people who parade both the masters and doctorate degrees did not earn them by themselves. Some stayed in their houses, especially, the very rich and the politicians, and pay university dons to write there dissertations and theses for them. At best, they attended classes sparingly, took the exams and obviously pass because sometimes the scripts they submitted were not the actual ones marked, because it is pre-arranged. But when it comes to the thesis, that's a different show altogether. It is completely paid for as a contract. A professor writes it, and they also make sure that such professors will be there for the defence whether it is the internal or external defence. That is how we now have mediocres who cannot speak any correct English earning masters and doctorate degrees. Can you now imagine what quality of lecturers men and women who earn these postgraduate degrees in this way would be? And they are already occupying high and exalted positions in our citadels of learning. A vicious cycle that recycles mediocrity and perpetuates it. What kind of university graduates would this class of lecturers produce. Of course their kind!

This does not even end here. It has even affected the promotion or appointment of professors in our universities.

That reminds me of one of our professors of the College of Health Sciences in the then university of Ife, Ile-Ife, Professor T. A. I. Grillo of blessed memory. A very pompous but erudite professor of Anatomy and Histochemistry. He was the person who actually pioneered the establishment of the then college of health sciences – as the Medical School in Ife University(now OAU) is called. He was a man who came from the family of great intellectuals, because about four other brothers of his as well as his wife, Baxter Grillo, were all professors, in Neurosurgery, fine arts and many other disciplines. His wife was in the same Anatomy department with him at Ife. He was nominated for Nobel prize in 1977 for a work he did on Insulin. When his own wife was to be made a professor, pompously he would say, what does she know to answer professor. He used to say that a lot of Nigerian professors were "Ikeja Professors". That was when the old Ikeja airport used to be the International airport in Nigeria. He meant to say that most of those professor could not be recognized outside the shores of Nigeria. He would tell us that once they got to the Ikeja airport, they would drop their professional garbs!

That was then! What of now? The situation has degenerated so badly. We now have all manner of professors. We have the ones that met the stipulated number and quality of publications by dent of hard work. We also have those who to a large extent plagiarized the papers with which they became professors. I know of a man, a one-time CMAC (Chairman Medical Advisory Committee) in a mainline teaching hospital East of the Niger who was forced to resign his appointment with the teaching hospital because they caught him in the web of plagiarism. He was said to have translated a publication in a

French Medical Journal and submitted as his own work. Actually, to have heard that he did that was not a surprise to a lot of us because he used to boast openly that since all that was needed was to submit papers he would one day do so no matter how he got them. So some of the papers he submitted, he plagiarized from other journals in other languages. Other publications of his were things he "knocked" together from here and there without carrying out any research of any form. He was a man that lacked scruples, completely bereft of integrity. So he could do anything for anything.

When his university forced him to resign, as a soft landing for him, instead of outright termination of his appointment, he did. But he still presented those same papers (publications) to his State university, and today he is a full-fledged professor. What a shame! And there are so many others like this man, wearing professional garbs but know little or nothing in their field. There are still those who do not have any publication at all, but because their institutions are working for recognition and relevance, especially those universities in the educationally backward parts of this nation as well as many privately owned universities, especially when these universities are preparing for accreditation of courses, they are appointed professors to fill in the gap. These are political professors. These are those who are in the good books or camp of the university's Vice Chancellor or authorities or would we say, those who are in his political camp. These ones are also promoted to the rank of professors to appease them, even when they do not yet qualify. This is the second group of political professors. The sad aspect of this is that even in the same universities, there are those academic minded lecturers who have actually researched and have produced more than enough quality papers (publications) even of international standards, but who have been kept "marking time"(stagnated) just because they are not in the good books of the powers that be. This is another way the heads of our higher institutions are emasculating academic excellence in those places. Instead of the good old adage of "publish or perish". It has been changed to "protest and perish".

Again, come to think about it, what was the pedigree of some of these men before they were appointed vice chancellors or rectors or whatever of these institutions. Despite the hogwash of university senate electing and sending names to the visitor of the university, that is the president (for Federal universities) or the Governor (in a State university), truth is that, it is all a manipulated thing from its beginning to the end because the prerogative is still that of the visitor to decide who to appoint even outside the nominees that were sent to him. Most of the time the appointment is based either on ethic or political party lines or some other factors, rather than excellence and integrity of the nominees. Or what else would motivate the president to appoint as vice chancellor, a man that was indicted as a commissioner in his state of origin, for corruption, and was even sacked from that position.

So we see that the whole problem of our educational rottenness goes down to the foundation. I have said it before, and will always say it again, and again that nobody erects a lasting edifice on a porous soil. My people have this adage that says: "whatever you get from the side of the pot goes to the side of the mouth". The computer world calls it "Garbage in, garbage out". Scripture says that "whatever a man sows, that he shall also reaps".

Always, the character of the kingdom emanates from the character of the king. The head cannot be insane and you expect the rest of the body to be sane. It is an impossibility. Like will always beget like. The offspring of the snake will be like the snake, longish. Don't forget, that we are talking about integrity here. It takes integrity to make the right appointment so that meritocracy will always be placed above mediocrity, because when you appoint somebody who is not fitted for a job purely because of ethnic, tribal or party affiliation despite obvious factors that should deter you from doing so, you have enthroned mediocrity at the expense of meritocracy. In doing what is wrong, you have already laid a very faulty foundation in that establishment. This has been one of the biggest setbacks to good and purposeful governance or leadership in the Nigerian nation.

Notice that the Bible says in 1 Tim. 5:18, *"Thou shall not muzzle the ox that treaded out the corn. And, the labourer is worthy of his reward".*

So when a governor fails to pay the wages of the workers (in this instance, the teachers), he creates a loophole for corrupt practices including exam papers leakages as well as things like SORTING and handout racketeering, because those teachers want to make ends to meet. Hence they have started indulging in these evil and corrupt practices and have come to see it as a way of making easy money. The situation has become so bad that even when you begin to pay them their wages, they find it difficult to stop. That is why for example, policemen on road-checks will never stop collecting bribe from transporters on the road even if you begin to pay a police constable a million naira a month. Why? Because it has permeated their whole system and has become a way of life for them to the extent that whoever is not practicing that illegality is seen as an odd man. Ask N. F. Ogbonna.(a retired police officer but now a preacher of the gospel of Jesus Christ).

06

THE PLACE OF INTEGRITY IN MARRIAGE

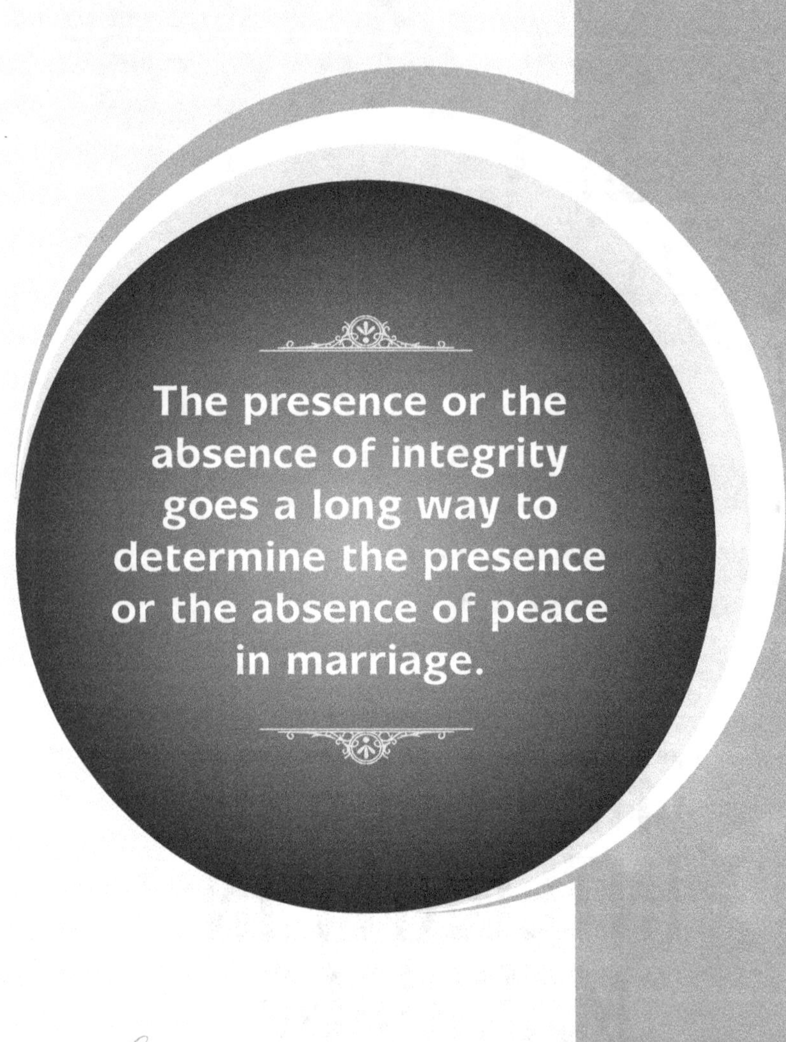
The presence or the absence of integrity goes a long way to determine the presence or the absence of peace in marriage.

Six

CHAPTER SIX

THE PLACE OF INTEGRITY IN MARRIAGE

Gen. 2"25;

"And they were both naked, the man and his wife and were not ashamed

Heb. 13:14;

"Marriage is honourable in all, and the bed undefiled; but whoremongers and adulterers God will judge".

Marriage is another very critical area where integrity has a very important role to play. Integrity is one of those major factors that will determine both the duration and enjoyment therein or the absence of both. A marriage that is established on integrity right from the beginning (courtship) of it, is most likely to last and be enjoyed

DURING COURTSHIP

Courtship is simply that period of time when two people, a man and a lady, who have agreed 'in principle" to marry, use to study or acquaint or familiarize with each other. It could last from as short as one month to as long as a few years. However, neither too short nor too long a courtship is timely helpful. Each could be hazardous. Some acclaimed experts in marriage have suggested that true courtship should be between six months and one year.

A well-handled courtship could go a long way to help make a marriage very healthy. A well- handled Christian courtship is one in which there is openness (excluding sexual intercourse), between the two people. Indeed integrity in marriage or the absence of it usually, but not always, starts during the courtship, even though some partners fell to pick it up at this time, either because they have been overwhelmed with love, which indeed could only be a make-believe thing like in movies, or there is so much pretense by either or both partners.

The time of courtship is a period when each partner should learn or know almost everything about the other person, if you like call it each other's biography. Partners should for example know the true age of each other, not the doctored one. I say this because I know of the case of a couple where it took the husband almost twenty-three years to know the true age of his wife – who kept using different dates until a time when the spirit of God persuaded her to tell him the truth! Eventually she was indeed older than her husband. Thank God, according to her husband, he absorbed the shock with equanimity. But you will agree with me that this issue that should have been taken care of during courtship, but wasn't. It could in some circumstances cause an upheaval in the marriage!

In the same vein, we have known of cases, even among professing Christians where either of the would be spouses failed to reveal a serious medical condition during courtship to the other and it turns out later to be a cog in the wheel of the progress of that marriage.

There have been situations where the man has erectile dysfunction (impotence) or is azospermic (zero sperm count), and he knows it! Yet he failed to tell the sister or lady. And she only finds out on the first night together after their wedding! You can imagine how devastating it could be! There have also been cases where a would-be bride never told her would-be groom, the gynaecological situations she had until after their wedding. Problems like uterine fibroid, amenorrhoea, and other such feminine problems. There have also been cases where genotypes have been lied about or doctored in collusion with a laboratory personnel, only to be discovered when the children start coming and you start seeing sicklers contrary to expectation. What peace do you think would be in the marriage when these sickle cell disease children are being taken in and out of hospital because of somebody's dishonesty!! We also have cases where one of the would-be spouses has a history of mental illness that was carefully hidden from the other until after marriage when it begins to manifest.

We have also known of cases where one of the would-be partners lied about their academic qualifications, or their real business or profession or even place of employment. There's this story of a young man who lied to a young lady about where he works. He told her that he works in an oil company, and he used every possible method to effectively cover the lie. It was after the wedding that the bubble burst, and this caused a rift in that marriage that has refused to settle.

We also have another instance where the young man told the lady who was a university graduate herself that he has a university bachelor's degree. Because he was privately employed, the lady could not find out that it was a lie. She only found out after close to two years in the marriage when things became tough in the man's business and ends were not meeting and his wife wanted to use her connection to secure a job for him in an institution and they demanded for the man's CV. He started telling stories. He actually had an OND (Ordinary National Diploma).This caused their separation for a while before peace was restored by intervention from relations.

These are all the problems the courtship period was expected to handle, but because of lack of integrity in courtship, they were not handled.

These give a wrong foundation to some marriages and can be recipes for constant misunderstanding, quarrels and even eventual divorce.

Marriage Proper

The presence or the absence of integrity goes a long way to determine the presence or the absence of peace in marriage. As I already discussed above, it could have its roots in the courtship but not always.

I referred to Gen. 2:25 at the beginning of this chapter. For emphasis, let us quote it again here: "And they were both naked, the man and his wife and were not ashamed". I am interested in the word "naked". It could mean the physical nakedness but that is not what am talking about. "Naked" here also means transparency. It could also mean honesty that makes up the word integrity. And it says "were not ashamed". It means when they are honest or transparent or truthful or faithful in their dealings with each other, they have nothing to fear. They have no reason to suspect each other. They have no reason to doubt each other. They will have no reason to want to outsmart each other: it's like saying as it is written in 1 Jn. 4:18, *"There is no fear in love; but perfect love casteth out fear; because fear hath torment. He that feareth is not made perfect in love".*

Note the first part of the verse: "There is no fear in love; but perfect love casteth our fear".

Perfect love brings peace. But do we have that today?

On the contrary, today a lot of marriages are bugged by such issues as; finances, extramarital relationships, meddling by parents or in-laws. Lack of submission, lack of provision, infertility, the children factor, unhealthy rivalry or competitiveness and so on. In fact it is legion. It cannot be exhausted here, neither am I competent to do so!

On finances

In our finances for example, where there is "nakedness" (transparence) if both spouses are the working class, they should know how much each of them earns at the end of the month or week as the case may be. And they should also know when salaries have been paid or not. I am not an apostle or advocate of a joint account, neither am I against it. If the couple truly and willingly decide to have a joint account, no problem. But I tilt more to the area of liberty for each spouse, that is, each person owns a separate account. However, they could agree on a contributory joint project account. I also believe that in such a joint account, each of the spouses should be a signatory. The joint salary account has turned some women into slaves to their husbands, and occasionally or rarely vice versa. It has also made some men very lazy especially when their wives earn more.

Spouses are not only to know what the other person earns, they should also know how and what money is being spent for. If either of the couples is involved in a monthly or weekly contribution, it should also be on agreement by the two of them. When I say they should know what money is being spent for, I don't mean every naira and kobo. But reasonable expenses as it relates to in-laws, some big purchases, big charities, or loans being given out to friends, and the like. If for no other reason, but for the reason of respect, courtesy and accountability. Sometimes, it could be painful to allow your partner to hear of such expenses from an external source. It could be seen as lack of respect or dishonesty and could lead to lack of trust which is a marriage killer.

Extra marital relationship

Again Heb. 13:4 says; *"Marriage is honourable, in all, and the bed undefiled; but whoremongers and adulterers, God will judge"*

The first thing to say here is that for every couple and most especially for believers, there should be no room at all for extra marital affairs, it is unacceptable and not allowed in Christianity. Adultery is sinful, and we are inexcusable. Spouses must therefore stay clear or flee from every relationship that may lure them into such illicit affairs. Whether it is business, professional, academic, social or religious relationships. We must not be ignorant of the devices of the devil especially in this age and generation when dressings have become very seductive, especially with the female gender.. We are also in an age of great permissiveness and moral bankruptcy.

One way of overcoming this is that couples must be as close as possible to each other on a daily basis if possible. They must also be able to openly communicate with each other the challenges they face from time to time with the opposite sex. But then, when your spouse is telling you such experiences, you must know the correct actions to take. You don't need to act irrationally or aggressively, else you can worsen the whole situation. There is the story of a woman who told her husband how her boss or is it her colleague in the place of work has been making sexual advances at her persistently. Her husband went and confronted the man and a fight that was disgraceful ensued between them. The matter led to a big rift between him and his wife and the wife decided never to inform him again of such things. We also have a situation where a man informed his wife of a woman, his client that was also making advances. His wife went straight and confronted the other woman and they had terrible altercations. That woman went and broadcast it to other women who were also clients of this man. However, the man's business unfortunately is centered mostly on women. Subsequently, the man was deserted by his clients because the story in town was; don't go there again. His wife is very aggressive. She sees every woman that comes to her husband as a potential mistress. And in the end, the matter terribly affected the marriage as the man now saw his wife as the enemy of his business.

So remember that it's out of the integrity of your spouse that he/she informed you of what he/she was passing through.

We must not as spouses abuse, ridicule or discourage each other's integrity by our attitudes. We should rather hail and encourage it. Otherwise what would happen is that when next your spouse has experiences out there in the market place, he/she will not share it with you. He/she may begin to bottle it up and that could in the long run endanger your relationship in marriage.

There is no doubt that we are in a world where nobody can be can island to himself. We cannot exist alone. We need other people to exist, to do business, to learn, to carry out assignments whether spiritual or secular. But we must make sure that we know the limits of our relationships out there. We should have standards to live by. Finally spouses should learn to trust each other and also to be trustworthy. Trust is an integral part of integrity. We must cast down imaginations and all forms of speculations.

INFERTILITY IN MARRIAGE

Infertility in marriage is a very thorny issue in marriage which if not well handled by both spouses could seriously endanger the marriage. It has led to many divorces and separations. Many times, it has resulted from impatience, ignorance, integrity issues and faithlessness. We must not also forget that God Himself can restrain a couple from bearing child for a season (see Gen.16:2 KJV) or even shut the womb like in the case of Hannah (1Sam.1:5). As I stated early, if the couple were sincere enough to each other during courtship, some of the things that eventually cause infertility could have been discussed and probably handled during that period . Why would a man hide a case of impotence, low sperm count or no sperm count at all (oligospermia or azospermia respectively) which he knows he suffers from during courtship, only for it to become the cause of infertility experienced after wedlock. And do you know that sometimes even when the man is totally aware of this, he will still blame the wife and refuses to submit himself for any laboratory investigations. He allows his wife to be harassed and embarrassed by members of his family subjecting the poor lady to all forms of both orthodox and unorthodox medications. There is this case of a former auxiliary nurse that once worked with me. They had been married for about four years and no child yet. One day as a doctor, I asked her if she and her husband had consulted with a gynaecologist. She said yes and that she has done all forms of investigations and the doctor said nothing was wrong with her. Then I asked if her husband has done any, she said no. On further enquiry, I found out that because the young man has had a child out of wedlock,therefore he believes that nothing is wrong with him because that child is an evidence that he is okay. I invited him, and after speaking with him, he was persuaded to go for seminal analysis. Behold the result showed that he was suffering from azospermia. You see, who even knows if he is indeed the father of that other child. After all, no DNA paternity test had been done.

On the other hand, why would a young lady who is amenorrheic (does not menstruate), or does not ovulate, or has a fibroid or blocked fallopian tubes, conceal this from the young man courting her for marriage even when she already knows about that health condition! These are all potential causes of infertility that should have been discussed during courtship and possibly handled before tying the nuptial knots.

The reason for discussing these issues before wedding is so that, if any of them is in doubt or does not have enough faith to handle these problems, he or she could withdraw, when it's still allowed and relatively harmless. It's not a must that every courtship must end in marriage. Concealing such health problems from the would-be spouse during courtship shows absence of integrity in relationship.

Again, I know that we make marriage vows during wedding ceremonies like "for richer, for poorer, in sickness and in health, until death do us part". Then, why should infertility, if there is integrity, cause a divorce or separation in marriage, especially in these days when we have various genuine options to have our own children in marriage which include, adoption, in-vitro fertilization, surrogacy and the like. There is even one that is called crypto-pregnancy. To me the details are shoddy and shady. But the point here is that there's no problem in marriage that we cannot surmount if we work and live with integrity.

07

INTEGRITY IN OUR FINANCES

Money matters right from the time of Christ Himself, proved to be a slippery issue that has swept many believers off their feet. If a believer has mastery over money matters, he will do very well in his Christian race.

Seven

CHAPTER SEVEN

INTEGRITY IN OUR FINANCES

"FOR THE LOVE OF MONEY IS THE ROOT OF ALL EVIL: WHICH WHILE SOME COVETED, THEY ERRED FROM THE FAITH, AND PIERCED THEMSELVES THROUGH WITH MANY SORROWS". (I Tim. 6:10, KJV).

One of the things that tests or manifests the integrity of a believer is the way that believer handles money matters. Money matters right from the time of Christ Himself, proved to be a slippery issue that has swept many believers off their feet. If a believer has mastery over money matters, he will do very well in his Christian race. The love of money destroyed Judas Iscariot. He was the treasurer in custody of the purse, and from time to time, he stole from it for his personal needs.

John. 12:6 (NLT) says "*...he, Judas, was a thief, and since he was in charge of the disciples' money, he often stole some for himself*". And this was why he became an easy accomplice with the Jewish leaders who were determined to kill the Lord Jesus. He betrayed his master for thirty pieces of silver. Matt. 26:15-16 reports *"Then Judas Iscariot, one of the twelve disciples, went to the leading priests and asked how much they would pay him to betray Jesus to them. And they gave him thirty pieces of silver. From that time on, Judas began looking for an opportunity to betray Jesus"*. That is what the love of money can do! Unfortunately he didn't even live to enjoy the money, because he eventually committed suicide. Matt. 27:5 says *"then Judas threw the silver coins down in the temple and went and hanged himself"*. What a miserable way to end his life after having followed Jesus for three years. He went straight to hell because nobody who commits suicide can ever enjoy eternity in heaven. This is because none of us has the power to take our own lives at will.

Another very painful and unfortunate story in the scriptures which displayed greed and lack of integrity in financial management is the story of Ananias and his wife Sapphira in Act. 5:1-10. This was at a time when the believers were united in heart and mind. Scriptures says that they felt that what they owned was not their own, so they shared everything they had (Act 4:32, 37). They sold their possessions and brought the money to the apostles. But Ananias and his wife Sapphira sold a property, and brought part of the money to the apostle, CLAIMING IT WAS THE TOTAL AMOUNT. (Act 5:1-2). This was the caveat. They could have said, of a truth, we brought only part, because nobody was compelled to bring all of it. But because they were greedy and lacked integrity, and yet desired to receive accolades they did not deserve, they lied to the Holy Ghost. And this caused them an untimely and disgraceful death.

We see from these two Bible stories, the betrayal of Jesus by Judas Iscariot, and his subsequent sudden death, and the story of Ananias and Sapphira's dishonesty in financial transaction which also led to their sudden shameful death that when the love of money makes us to go contrary to the will of God, we may not live long enough to enjoy that ill-gotten wealth. That is where Jeremiah. 17:11 comes true. That scripture says *"Like a partridge that hatches eggs she has not laid, so are those who get wealth by unjust means. At midlife they will lose their riches in the end, they will become poor old fools"* (NLT). Judas never lived to enjoy the ill-gotten thirty pieces of silver, instead he returned it and yet died, both physically and spiritually (Rev. 21:8). In the same manner, the money Ananias and his wife Sapphira greedily left behind was never enjoyed by them and they died very untimely and twice. The Lord Jesus asked in Matt. 16:26, Mk. 8:36, and Lk. 9:25, *"for what shall it profit a man, if he shall gain the whole world, and lose his own soul"*. Financial greed or insatiability or dishonesty is fast eroding the fabrics of our Christian faith.

Many believers have lost their integrity because of money. This happens in many ways as buttressed by the following stories.

About 1997, when I was the president of a chapter of our fellowship (FGBMFI), a wealthy member of our chapter, now of blessed memory brought the sum of twenty thousand naira (N20,000.00) when Naira had value, that would amount to more than a million naira today. He asked us to use it as a revolving loan of five thousand naira maximum for beneficiaries at no interest to the lowly placed or financially incapacitated members. They were expected to return the loan after a few months without interest, so that it could be given to others who also needed it. We quickly put some people in charge of the money/loans. One condition was that whosoever needed to borrow, should have another member of the fellowship as surety in case he fails to return the money.

People quickly came and collected the loans. I even was a surety for a brother and friend who incidentally also attended the same church with me. 90% of the people who collected this loan defaulted, that is, they neither came to repay it at all, nor did their sureties do so. Even my friend and brother in the same church when the heat came too much on me reminding me that the person I stood surety for had not repaid; remember that at that time I was the chapter president, I approached him in the church one day after Sunday service, he became so antagonistic and even pugnacious. Our pastor was close that day and was watching what was happening between us and intervened. But it was not that this brother was not yet buoyant enough to repay this money, and this was happening, more than five years after he took that loan. So I never asked him of that money again. And he never paid it.

And that was how that revolving interest-free loan ended. The whole money disappeared in the pockets of borrowers.

We also had another young man then, who had just lost his job with the bank, in those days when banks were sacking their staff for all sorts of frivolous reasons. This man had just joined our chapter and was also attending our intercessory prayers on Mondays. So one of those days he ran to us at the fellowship to inform us that his landlord had just thrown him and his family out of their accommodation because of their inability to settle their rent since he lost his job with the bank. And at that time, his wife was nursing a baby of a few months old. He was in serious distress because his family was almost sleeping in an uncomfortable place with a few months old baby.

I did not have any personal loan to give, but I consulted with some officers of our chapter including our treasurer and we agreed to give him a loan since he had found a new accommodation. He packed into the new accommodation. With time, things got better for him, he got a new job, and even replaced his car. His wife who is a qualified nurse, also secured a job in a reputable hospital. We reminded him of the need to repay the loan, he keep promising he would do so, but after a period, he stopped coming to fellowship. Even when he stopped coming, I met him a couple of times and reminded him that it was God's money that we gave him because of his difficult condition then. But to my greatest surprise, he has not done so up till today. His wife has since secured a job in a federal health institution, but they never paid back the loan.

What of my close Christian brother, though not of my church but worships in another reputable Pentecostal church. In 1997, he was rushed to my clinic as an emergency case. His sickness was almost unto death, and I guess it probably got that bad because he was going through some financial challenges, being a transporter, and his vehicle had broken down for some time. So some friends brought him to me. I admitted him even without paying the card fee. I treated him, and to the glory of God, within a week he was healed and was discharged. He promised to come to pay as soon as he repaired his bus and was on the road again. Of course I allowed him to go. Not a dime was paid for either investigations or treatment. After a few months, I noticed that he was on the road again, I granted him what I call a moratorium, even for up to six months. I waited and I never saw him. When I eventually contacted him about my money he said he had just bought a second bus and so was low in cash, but promised to come and pay when things improved. I never saw him, and I am yet to see him, more than twenty years after. He has been avoiding me since them. But can he avoid God?

I have multiples of examples of this kind of brethren who have no integrity when it comes to paying what they borrowed or what they owe. Scriptures says in Rm. 13:8, *"Owe no man anything, but to love one another"*.

Ps. 37:21 says *"The wicked borroweth, and payeth not again…"*.

So it is an act of wickedness and injustice to owe or borrow and not pay back. But these scenarios I painted above are rampant among believers today. It happens in many forms. Some come to you in their desperate moments to ask for financial help in the form of loan so they can pay their house rents that have long expired, some need to pay their children's school fees, other may need to settle medical bills or need to repair their grounded vehicles, or for an avalanche of other reasons. These reasons have become more frequent in the present day situation of wicked mis-governance when especially state and local governments are owing civil servant arrears of salaries for upward of twenty four months, and do not even remember pensioners at all. Some have retired for upward of four years and nobody has remembered them at all in terms of paying monthly pensions what more gratuities.

However, the sad thing is that this person who came to borrow and promised vehemently that he/she will return the money as soon as they are paid, or as soon as they receive the money they are expecting, never ever fulfill their promises. When the money comes, they disappear into oblivion, they begin to avoid you. Many times, they have used the money for another thing. They have forgotten that they made a promise. And to worsen the situation, they don't even call or come to explain their inability to pay back. They leave you to continue to wait and expect them until you are tired. This is where integrity is involved.

Prov. 6:2 says "thou art snared with the words of thy mouth, thou art taken with the words of thy mouth". Some other so called brethren go to buy from their brethren, and promise to soon come to pay, but they never ever do. Or sometimes if they asked for a few days or weeks, it takes either months or years before they ever do. And that will be after the matter may have taken another dimension. Sometimes, especially Christian sisters, go to collect clothings, they don't even need at that time, or even for the trending asoebi, and accumulate debts that one or two months salaries cannot pay because of covetousness or lack of contentment. This leads them into lies and debts. But 1 Tim. 6:6 says *"But godliness with contentment is great gain"*.

This particular scenario has different dimensions; brethren go to borrow to buy big SUV's, or cars they cannot maintain from paltry salaries or lean financial resources. Some go to rent expensive accommodations they do not need and cannot continue to pay for after the initial one or two year payment. Most of the time, this results from unhealthy competition with other brethren or siblings. They don't have a special fund or income they are expecting from which they will complete and continue payments subsequently or to carry out the routine maintenance that will obviously be needful with time. They are just believing that God will continue to provide. There is nothing wrong with believing God for provision, but the scripture says we must not be covetous (Rm. 7:7, Ex. 20:17). And that we must prophesy according to the measure of our faith. Some of the things that have terribly caused lack of financial integrity in our lives are greed, or lack of contentment, unhealthy competitions and indiscipline in financial management. These vices get worse when a man does not have the fear of the Lord again.

It is greed and lack of the fear of God that makes a public servant or a politician in a leadership position to embezzle public fund that is kept in his care to execute projects for the people.

It is greed and the absence of the fear of God that leads a public officer to over invoicing, to padding of budgets and demanding 10-90% kickback from contractors.

It is financial recklessness or indiscipline that makes public officers, governors, heads of institutions to misuse the monies meant for payment of salaries and pensions, for other frivolous things, for partying, reckless drinking, political settlements and womanizing.

This absence of financial integrity has also greatly affected and afflicted the church to the extent that in many places preaching is now skewed toward how to extort money from the members by dubiously misinterpreting the word, giving manipulated prophecies, words of wisdom and words of knowledge. There is now serious manipulation of figures in accounting in the church by both accounting officers and ministers in the church with connivance at times between ministers and church treasurer when both of them are gullible and same minded.

I had earlier in this book told you the story of the pastor whose treasurer was robbed in his house. As I said, at that time, the treasurer had some church money that was in his house, but he securely hid it somewhere, so when the robbers took every other money in that house, they could not see that one. When the treasurer informed the pastor later that robbers came to his house, he excitedly told him that the church money was intact. The treasurer was dumbfounded and greatly embarrassed when the pastor asked him to inform the church that the money was also stolen, so that both of them, pastor and the treasure, could share it!! That was what made the treasurer to leave the church.

Another friend of mine narrated to me how he disappointedly left his church too. He said he joined the church more than six years before. And after some time he was appointed into the leadership of the place. He noticed consistently that there was never a time the church finances had ever been brought for discussion. The pastor only talked about finances when he wanted to raise money. So, in some meetings, he was the only one bold to ask if there was no provision for rendering of account to the leadership or membership. The pastor would always parry the question. He said in one occasion, the pastor came to him privately and harshly told him to desist from asking about the church finances, saying that the matter was to be left between him and God alone. In fact he told him that if he did not like it that way, he should find his way out of the place. And that was exactly what he did.

In another Pentecostal church a while ago, according to a prominent member, they came for Holy Communion service. Sometime during the service, when everybody was set to come to receive communion, the man of God, paused for a while, and then announced that he had just heard from the Holy Spirit, that whosoever wants to receive the Holy Communion should come with an offering or else should forget about it. My friend said that he and some others who did not believe it, including those who did not have the amount the pastor mentioned, were denied the Holy Communion that day. I have also personally experienced something like that. But let me stop that there.

There is this story told by a very respectable man of God; A General Overseer of a ministry invited some two other ministers to be part of few days of revival service he organized. One of the days during the ministrations, these two visiting ministers announced that they were led to raise an offering for orphans and the needy. People trooped out to give. The offerings were gathered specially and handed over to them. Throughout that night, the G.O did not hear them discuss with him how the fund would be handled. The following day before they left, he asked them that he was still expecting them to discuss with him how the offering for the orphans would be handled. To his surprise, they laughed at him and told him that they had already handled the whole thing. They told him that both of them had lost their parents, and so they were the orphans and the needy. So they had shared the money. What will you call this?

Recently, a friend, and an elder in a foremost Pentecostal church narrated to me how an elder in his church misused the money another church member entrusted in his hands for safe keep. He used the money for betting and eventually lost and when the friend came to collect that money, he began to tell cock and bull stories!! And the matter was eventually reported to the church leadership. Stories of that kind of betrayal of trust abound today even among the so called born again believers.

But I remember vividly that my late father who had no

claim to being born again, but who had the fear of God was a banker to many people in the village even as a mere primary school teacher. I never knew of anytime any of those who trusted him with their monies came to collect them and got disappointed despite the fact that he was a poor primary school teacher with a myriad of problems including too many children to cater for. It was not an excuse to lose his integrity in financial management.

Today, especially in the so called Pentecostal churches, all sorts of seed faiths have been introduced by pastors, all in the bid to get money out of their congregants. You have seed faith to begin a new month, seed faith to end the month, seed faith to begin a week, seed faith to be a partaker of a beautiful testimony, seed faith for promotion, seed faith for getting a good marriage partner. We can go on and on. These seed faiths are totally different from the regular church offerings, and tithe. Also totally different from welfare collection. They are different from sowing for church journals. So on one Sunday, a member may have given up to seven or eight kinds of offerings. And this has become a deterrent to many members from going to church. Any Sunday they don't have enough for the various offerings and seed faiths, they prefer to stay at home than to go to church to embarrass themselves. Because sometimes, if you are seated there in church, and don't go out to give, people, including the ministers begin to think of all sorts of thing about you including thinking that you are stingy.

This way, the greed and lack of financial integrity of some ministers have made many members to stay away from worshipping God, and some have completely backslidden. And one obvious truth is that most of these seed faiths go into the pastor's pocket. They are not accounted for like the routine offerings and tithes.

In some congregations, the pastor details a member whose duty it is to make sure that these monies are quickly kept away for the "Man of God".

Must a so called man of God introduce all sorts of prangs in order to swindle the membership to satisfy his greed. Or do we mean that God never rewards adequately again? No, it is greed, and avarice resulting from an unhealthy competition with his contemporaries coupled with lack of contentment that leads these pastors and others into this kind of evil. When they see some other pastors with SUVs or living in beautiful mansions, they begin to desire same, not even minding that those ones have probably paid the prize in ministry and have genuinely acquired those things. That is why the Bible says in Prov. 28:20[b] that *"he that maketh haste to be rich shall not be innocent"*.

It is this same hastiness in making wealth even by the very young people in their early twenties that has in recent times led to armed robberies, kidnapping, advanced fee fraud (aka 419) and now all forms of ritual killings and harvesting the organs of both innocent and gullible people for ritual money.

The most disturbing aspect or dimension of these acts of ritual killing is the one that involves the so called ministers of the gospel who covenant with the devil in many ways to prosper their church, but indeed their pockets. Some have gone to purchase talisman and all forms of fetish demonic objects or substances from evil priests which they use to mesmerize and charm their members, and so turning them into "robots" who do their biddings like zombies without thinking. With these charms they are taking over their members properties including cars and houses. They have also drained them to the level of penury or bankruptcy with these charms. In some instances they have taken over their wives also. Some of these so called men of God have even laid the foundation of their church buildings with the blood of some human beings. A few years ago, in the southern part of this country, bodies of some young men were found in the foundation of a so-called church building, being erected!! What is the sole aim of all this? Is it not to be seen to be "powerful"? Working magic in the name of miracles and then pulling crowds that will do their biddings and eventually making them stupendously rich?

Again the Holy Spirit reminds me of Jere. 17:11 and Prov. 13:11.

Jere. 17:11 says *"As the partridge sitteth on eggs and hatchet them not,so he that getteth riches, and not by right, shall leave them in the midst of his days, and at the end shall be a fool"*.

Prov. 3:11 says *"wealth gotten by vanity shall be diminished; but he that gathereth by labour shall increase"* (KJV). NLT calls it *"wealth from get-rich-quick schemes"*.

FROM WHERE DID HE GET THAT MONEY?

Many years ago, I heard an authentic story of a minister of the gospel I know very well because we schooled in the same university, Great Ife, how one of his members came on a particular service and donated a huge sum of money. The man of God thanked him then but asked him to have a discussion with him (the pastor) after service.

When they met after the service, the pastor who knows him very well and what he does for a living, asked him how he came about such a huge sum of money. The young man got very annoyed and called it an insult. He said he thought the pastor was calling him to appreciate him specially for the donation to the church. He refused to disclose the source of such sudden wealth to the man of God. The pastor in turn told him point blank that if he would not tell him the source, he in turn would not accept it. So he took it immediately and handed it back to him. The young man stormed out of the church and never returned. But the pastor had peace. And the returning of that money did not stop them from completing the project, because God remains the owner of the cattle on a thousand hills.

There is also a story that made news and went viral some years ago. This also had to do with a young man that suddenly began to donate huge sums of money to his church far beyond his earnings. This was in the church of a mainline Pentecostal minister. The minister himself knew about this sudden affluence of this member, but he never cared to ask him, rather each time he brought such huge sums, he just blessed him and even began to praise him for his generosity.

But, the company where he was working was haemorrhaging financially and was frantically investigating the source of that financial haemorrhage, until it was traced to that young man, and he was promptly arrested. That was when the whole story was unearthed, and it became a huge scandal for the man of God and his church because it was proved that he knew about it all but never asked.

Today, all kind of money flocks into our churches, both orthodox and Pentecostal, and hardly does any minister try to find out how some of them that are obviously suspicious came about their wealth. Monies from ritual killings, advanced fee fraud (a.k.a 419), prostitution, armed and other forms of robbery. High level of corruption, drug trafficking, etc, are flowing into our churches and the ministers are highly excited receiving them, and showering enconiums on the donors, and giving them exalted places in the church, and even handing out titles like, Elder, Deacon, Deaconess, Knight, Mother or Father in Israel, Worthy son, Worthy daughter, Ezinne, Ezinna, Ezi-ada and all the like to these men, and women. These titles have now become what can be bought with money, and is reserved for the highest bidders.

A lot of titles have been invented in our churches to deceive gullible men and women who think that paying and garnering titles are a sure and short way to make heaven.

This is a subtle way of taking us back to the early days of the church when the priests taught the congregants about purgatory – a place, waiting place, from which people who died in sin can move from to heaven depending on how much money their living relations can release for the priests to celebrate masses for them. But these ignorant and gullible relations believed it all and kept requesting for masses upon masses. But that was in the days of obvious darkness to the word of God. It was even an abomination to see anybody who was not a priest read the Bible. Even the man, William Tyndale (1494-1536) an English biblical scholar and linguist, a man that became a leading figure in the Protestant Reformation, who dared to translate the Bible into English language paid for it with his life. He was executed for that effort.

But what of today, when the Bible is now everywhere in every gadget, in numerous versions.

So today, because of the quest for money, congregants are being deceived and souls are being lost to hell fire, all because of lack of financial integrity. Compare what is happening today with what happened in Act. 8:17-21, when, Simon the Sorcerer was trying to entice the Apostles (Peter and John) with money so that he may receive the power to lay hands and people would receive the baptism of Holy Ghost. We are told in Act. 8:18-21 that " *...when Simon saw that through laying on of the apostles hands the Holy Ghost is given, he offered them money, saying, give me also this power that on whomsoever I lay hands, he may receive the Holy Ghost. But Peter said unto him, thy money perish with thee, because thou hast thought that the gift of God may be purchased* *with money. Thou hast neither, part nor lot in this matter: for thy heart is not right in the sight of God".*

This was when ministers had integrity, and were not pecuniary minded.

However, today a whole lot of the ministers themselves are going to occult shrines with money to purchase power so that whosoever they lay their hands on will fall under the "anointing" demonic anointing. That is the level of decadence and debasement we have got to craving for financial gratifications. These so-called men of God are no longer waiting for God to pay them. They are paying themselves because they are in a haste to make wealth (Prov. 28:20b).

One very important virtue a believer or minister of God must possess is contentment, which the scriptures says that, together with godliness, is a great gain. Financial greed, unhealthy competitions, obsessive love for money, and insatiability has eroded the very fabrics and roots of our faith. It has introduced all forms of vices into the church of Jesus Christ to the extent that what is now used to judge growth of a minister or ministry is the material possessions he and his ministry have, in terms of cars, houses, schools, hospitals, universities, private jets, gigantic church auditorium, and not the number of souls, or spiritual exploits like healings, miracles, and activation of other spiritual gifts during church activities or other events like crusades.

My honest assertion or conclusion is that any true believer or minister of the gospel who for pecuniary reasons becomes manipulative, fraudulent, occultic, or compromising in one way or the other does not indeed know or understand the way and means of God. He does not have any faith in God at all.

I so much cherish what King David said in Ps. 37:25. He said, *"I have been young, and now am old; yet have I not seen the righteous forsaken nor his seed begging bread"*.

God indeed will never forsake His own because His name is FAITHFULNESS. He is a rewarder of them that diligently seek Him (Heb. 11:6b). The whole earth is the Lords, even the fullness thereof, the world and even all that dwell therein (Ps. 24:1).

He said in Ps. 50:10. *"for every beast of the forest is mine, and the cattle upon a thousand hills"*.

In Deut. 8:18, He said, *"But thou shall remember the LORD thy God; for it is he that giveth thee power to get wealth..."* He is the possessor of heaven and earth (Gen. 14:19). In Heb. 13:5, He said *"I will never leave thee, nor forsake thee"*.

James. 1:17 says *"Every good gift and every perfect gift is from above, and cometh down from the Father of lights, with whom is no variableness, neither shadow of turning"*.

These scriptures above tell you about His nature, His personality, His absoluteness, His resilience, His dependability, His inexhaustible possessions, His totalitarian control, His invincibility, His omniscience, omnipotence, His omnipresence. Buchi, the gospel musician, will say "Omni everything"!!

Therefore He is not fickle, not capricious, not chameleonic, not amnesic and not blinded. So whatever He says He will do, He surely will because He neither lacks the resources nor the ability to execute. Imagine what it means to be the possessor of heaven and earth!

Besides in Jere. 29:11, He said *"for I know the thoughts that I think towards you, said the Lord, thoughts of peace, and not of evil to give you an expected end"*

If therefore a believer, and a so called man of God knows and understands all that I have stated above about the ability of God to fully take care of all our needs, then why should we insist on cutting corners and defiling ourselves in order to possess material wealth? The answer is greed, avarice and impatience, which are obvious signs of lack of integrity.

Beloved remember what the Preacher said in Prov. 14:12 and Prov. 16:25: *"There is a way that seemeth right unto a man, but the end thereof are the ways of death"*.

Again don't forget Jere. 17:11. *"As partridge sitheth on eggs, and hatches them not, so he that getheth riches, and not by right, shall leave them in the midst of his days, and at the end shall be a fool"*.

But Ps. 37:4 says, *"Delight thyself in the Lord and He shall give thee the desires of thine heart"*.

Let us practice integrity in our finances because it pays handsomely and peacefully.

08

HOW DO WE GET INTEGRITY?

We must note that eternity can only be spent in one place. If we meet God's standard of holiness and purity till the end, then we will spend eternity with our God and the saints.

Eight

CHAPTER EIGHT

HOW DO WE GET INTEGRITY?

We can as believers become men and women of integrity by three major ways.

1. THE FEAR OF THE LORD
2. HAVING A PILGRIM CONSCIOUSNESS
3. FEEDING ON THE WORD OF GOD

We shall attempt to discuss them one after the other, as God enables us to do.

THE FEAR OF THE LORD

What do we exactly mean when we talk of the fear of the Lord? Is it like a child being afraid of a masquerade? Or being afraid of fire, or height, or darkness or such like things. I don't honestly think so. When we say we are afraid of the aforementioned things, all we tend to mean is that they scare us or that they make us to panic. But would the Lord scare us or make us panicky? No, it should rather be the opposite!

Whereas whatever scares us, makes us lose courage, but the presence of Lord strengthens our courage. Therefore the fear of the Lord could never mean the presence of a scare or the absence of courage.

So then what exactly do we mean when we talk about the fear of the Lord?

Maybe we should begin by quoting some of the Bible passages or verses that talk about the fear of the Lord, especially the more popular ones.

1. Deut. 6:2 ***"Fear the Lord thy God****, to keep all his statutes and his commandments, which I command thee..."*

2. Deut. 10:12- *"and now, Israel, what does the Lord thy God require of thee, but to FEAR THE LORD thy God, to walk in all His ways, and to love him, and to serve the Lord thy God with all thy heart, and with all thy soul".*

3. Josh. 24:14- *"Now therefore* ***fear the Lord****, and serve him in sincerity and in truth; and put away the gods which your fathers served on the other side of the flood, and in Egypt and serve ye the Lord".*

4. Job. 28:28:- *"And unto man he said, behold THE FEAR OF THE LORD, that is wisdom; and to depart from evil is understanding".*

5. Ps. 19:9- *"THE FEAR OF THE LORD is clean, enduring forever the judgments of the Lord are true and righteous altogether".*

6. Ps. 110:10- *"THE FEAR OF THE LORD is the beginning of wisdom"* (See Prov. 1:7)

7. Prov. 18:13 -*"THE FEAR THE LORD is to hate evil: pride and arrogance, and the evil way, and the forward mouth, do I hate"*.

8. Prov. 14:27- *"THE FEAR OF THE LORD is a fountain of life, to depart from the snares of death"*.

9. PROV. 15:16- *"Better is little with THE FEAR OF THE LORD than great treasure and trouble therewith"*.

10. Prov. 16:6 -*"By the mercy and truth iniquity is purged: and by FEAR OF THE LORD men depart from evil"*.

11. Prov. 19:23-*"THE FEAR OF THE LORD tendeth to life: and he that hath it shall abide satisfied; he shall not be visited with evil"*.

From all the above Bible verses dealing on THE FEAR OF THE LORD, we can comfortably deduce that THE FEAR OF THE LORD is to:

- ❖ To keep His statutes and commandments.
- ❖ To walk in all His ways and to love Him and serve Him with all our hearts.
- ❖ To serve Him in sincerity and truth, and have nothing to do with idolatry in all forms
- ❖ To walk in wisdom, knowledge and understand

- ❖ To hate and depart from every form of evil, and eschew pride and arrogance
- ❖ To live in contentment of what we have.

A man or believer that is fervently and ardently serving the Lord, being very mindful of God's words – dos and don'ts, a believer that is very contented with the little he/she has and does not compromise to add to what he/she possesses can only be a believer who hungers for integrity.

Lack of contentment, that is greed, is one of the major reasons why believers and unbelievers alike are in a rat race for accumulation of riches. This is the reason why ministers of the gospel are stealing from church fund and manipulating figures. It is the reason many ministers are even bribing to get better postings and plum positions from their superiors.

It has even affected the type of preaching that come from many pulpits – manipulative and brain-washing heresies – that are akin to dipping hands into the gullible and unsuspecting members pockets to get money. It is the reason there are all forms of false prophesies. At the extremes of it, the so called men of God have even gone to the devil in many forms to receive counterfeit power to hypnotize their members, all in the process of deceiving them for pecuniary interest and other purposes. All these depict total lack of integrity because they do not have the fear of the Lord.

So we can adduce from all the foregoing that the fear of the

Lord means reverential worship, total obedience, humility and yieldedness to the Lord (Jesus, who is God).

Josh. 24:14 says *"Now therefore, fear the Lord, and serve him in sincerity and in truth, and put away the gods which your fathers served on the other side of the flood"*. Sincerity, truthfulness are all integral part of integrity. Sincerity in business, sincerity in the place of work, sincerity in the home, selflessness in service.

Note, that scripture also talks about putting away "the gods". Remember that the word of God or rather the first commandment says *"thou shall not worship any other god beside me"*. And we call the worship of any other god idolatry. We also know that whatever else that takes away our attention from worshiping the true God in spirit and in truth is regarded as idolatrous.

The truth is that many things or rather many 'gods' are hampering our true worship of God. These include, the pursuit for riches, fame, political offices, fashion, property, professional engagements, family leanings, traditions of men and cultural beliefs. All these can constitute 'gods' in our lives depending on how we handle them, and how we prioritize them.

Many believers have seriously compromised their faith and eroded their integrity by their quest to get any of the good things of life. Note that the pursuit of none of the above is wrong in itself because it is the will of God to prosper us on all sides (see Jere 29:11, Deut. 8:18, Prov. 8:18). But it is when we give them undue priority and attention that they negatively affect and erode our Christian values and virtues that the danger comes. For example, the pursuit to make money is not evil, because after all without it, we cannot meet our personal needs and even Christian obligations. After all Eccl. 10:19[b] says *"but money answereth all things"*.

However, 1 Tim. 6:10 says *"for the LOVE of money is the root of all evil: which while some covet after, they have erred from the faith, and pierced themselves through with many sorrows"*. Note that it did not say *"for money is the root of all evil"* – rather it says the LOVE of it. "Love" there means an obsessive and uncontrolled desire for it that drives the individual to do just anything including stealing, killing, illicit drug peddling, defrauding, and bribery. The man or woman that has the fear of God will do none of such things above because of money. He will remember that godliness with contentment is great gain (1 Tim. 6:6) and that the little the righteous has is blessed of God. Therefore he will not make haste to be rich because such haste makers shall never be innocent (Prov. 28:20).

Another thing that is a symptom or sign of the lack of the fear of God is covetousness. That is why Jesus in Lk. 12:15 says, "take heed, and beware of covetousness: for a man's life consisteth not in the abundance of the things which he possesseth. Covetousness can be described as an inordinate desire for material or non-material possessions, especially, those of another individual. It stems from insatiability and greediness. Indeed, the vanity in being covetous is captured in Eccl. 5:10-11 which says: *"He that loveth silver shall not be satisfied with silver, nor he that loveth abundance with increase: this is also vanity. When goods increase, they are increased that eat them: and what good is there to the owners thereof, saving the beholding of them with their eyes?"* Covetousness is a major challenge today both in the church and in the world. And it has greatly eroded the integrity of the church. Worldliness has also become a great foe of the church and it appears many Christians (irrespective of how long they have been in the faith), are being carried along.

One dangerous aspect of worldliness is the competitiveness in it, the vanity of trying to impress or outclass each other in perishable material possessions. And this comes with the erosion of our innocence and sincerity. That's why the Preacher in Prov. 28:20 says that *"he that maketh haste to be rich shall not be innocent"*. Simply put, you will lose your character of integrity if you are in this vain chase of materialism. May God give us the understanding, to know that the true fear of God the Lord does not permit this,

HAVING A PILGRIM CONSCIOUSNESS

Jim Reeves sang a song I always remember its lyrics with trepidation. He said

"This world is not my home,
Am just passing through
My treasure are laid up
Somewhere beyond the blue

The Angels beckon me
From Heaven's open door

And I can't feel at home
In this world anymore.

Oh Lord, you know
I have no friend like you
If Heaven is not my home
Then Lord what will I do

The Angels beckon me
From Heaven's open door
And I can\t feel at home
In this world anymore...

That was a song from a man that had a pilgrim consciousness. Jim Reeves in this song fully realized that he was not of this world but rather what could be called a passerby. He realized that he had only limited time in this world. And indeed no man can live here forever. Even if we stay to a hundred and twenty years as the Bible said, we still shall surely one day pass on to eternity. So as Jesus said in His valedictory address in John 17:16, they are not of the world even as I am not of the world. Christ was speaking to His disciples which all of us that have received Him in spirit and in truth are. So we are passers-by.

1 Tim. 6:7 says *"for we brought nothing into this world, and it is certain we carry nothing out"*. Naked we came, and naked we will go.

A pilgrim is like a traveler. A true traveler always likes to travel light because it makes the journey faster and simple. It removes many encumbrances. Adam Smith, one of the greatest Economists of his time, said that a man of all luggage is the most difficult to travel. On the funny side of it, have you seen Nigerians in international airports struggling with luggage. Sometimes I think we indeed typify the "man of all luggage". That's by the way. But the truth is that the attitude of many of us, even believers, to the cares of this world – acquiring lands, buildings, cars, multiple business, receiving titles, and fighting bitterly and unchristianly for positions, shows that we have forgotten that we are mere pilgrims in this world. And a lot of us do this at a great compromise. Remember Prov. 28:20.

See also what Jere. 17:11 says *"As the partridge sitteth on eggs, and hatcheth them not; so he that getteth riches, and not by right, shall leave them in the midst of his days, and at his end shall be a fool"*. (KJV). This scripture gives me the goose pimples!

Mind you once again, we are not saying that acquiring wealth is not good. No, after all the Bible says that the riches of the gentiles shall be ours.

But when we go after these riches as if that is all we are here for, even when we know that some of these riches or the pursuit of them will lead us to great compromise or the eroding of our primary aim of being here to worship Him, that is where the problem lies.

For example, in the medical circles, today, there is an exodus of medical doctors to Saudi Arabia because of the jumbo salary they are paying compared to the pittance we get in Nigeria.

But we know that churches are not allowed to operate in that country, not to talk of evangelizing.

So for a born Christian doctor to go there to work, he does not only have to think in terms of the money primarily, but he has to think of what will happen to his faith if he stays a full year or two or even more without enjoying co-operate worship. He should not forget the injunction in Heb. 10:25 that says *"Not forsaking the assembling of ourselves together, as the manner of some is; but extorting one another and so much the more, as ye see the day approaching"*.

But I have seen many believers even without asking God if they should go, just leave for that country.

When you ask them, how they will manage this situation, they will tell you that they will be doing online or internet worship. Yeah thank God for internet worship, we all tested it during the lockdown occasioned by COVID-19. It could be manageable for a while, but nothing compares with the physical worship with the brethren.

Remember that Prov. 27:17 says *"Iron sharpeneth iron: so a man sharpeneth the countenance of his friend"*. These sharpening we receive from friends during corporate worship are some of the ways we acquire integrity in our lives.

If one then has the pilgrim consciousness, he will realize that allowing the quest for riches, titles and position at the expense of his faith is nothing but vanity and vexation of the spirit because one day you will abandon them and you may not be in a position to know how they will be managed after you have gone.

Having a pilgrim consciousness means that whatever you are doing here on earth, you always have it at the back of your mind that you are just here for a temporary period; that you are just passing through like Jim Reeves sang in that song. You also realize the fact that when you leave here, you have left forever and that you will never again have any knowledge of how whatever you left behind will be handled, neither would you again be in a position to determine how it is handled.

Having a pilgrim consciousness is therefore a restraining factor because it determines and even modulates the person's quest for riches, position and power.

Another important aspect of pilgrim consciousness is to remember what the scripture says in Heb. 9:27; *"And as it is appointed unto men once to die, but after this the judgment"*. I have already discussed the first part of that scripture that says that *"it is appointed unto men ONCE TO DIE"*. Once you are dead, you are dead forever. Somebody said you are "DEADED". That is you will never return here on earth in that form again. That is, there is nothing like reincarnation, as some preach about. You will never come back either as human, some other animal or tree! Once you are dead and buried, you are gone forever! Don't ever be deceived by any pundit of reincarnation.

However, my greater interest now is in the sec*ond part of Heb. 9:27, that says* "but after this the judgment".

There is a judgment day for each and every one of us. Matt. 12:36 says *"But I say unto you, that every idle word that men shall speak, they shall give account thereof in the day of judgment"*.

So the slogan “man die, go and get rotten” is not correct, but rather deceitful. Man is a tripartite being, made up of the body, the soul and the spirit. What dies actually and gets rotten is the body (flesh) but the soul and the spirit will actually face the judgment of God. This is why it is so unfortunate that some people go and commit suicide thinking that their problems are over. This is another deceit of the enemy. If you commit suicide, you have only compounded your problems and torment because you will go straight into everlasting torment.

Paul said in 2 Cor. 5:11 *“Knowing therefore the terror of the Lord, we persuade men...”*

If we know that taking our own lives will worsen things eternally for us, then we should never do it. In the same vein, if we know that, there is a judgment that will come after this life, we don't ever need anybody to persuade us to order our steps circumspectly here with great dexterity of faith and integrity. We cannot therefore afford to live carelessly as if everything ends here. We all have an account to render to our Maker, at the end of this life and in fact we shall be inexcusable as Rm. 2:1 says. This is because if we think that we have a compelling reason to have behaved in a particular way that is not pleasing to God, on that day, God will bring some other persons who faced similar situations, yet overcame.

If you say it was barrenness that made you do whatever evil you did, God will call Abraham and ask him how many years he and Sarah were barren, and yet they kept their integrity and overcame.

If you say you were seduced into whatever, He will bring Joseph to testify how many times Potiphar's wife tried to seduce him, yet he stood his ground. If you say you were in captivity, He will bring the three Hebrew young men, Shadrach, Meshach and Abednego, who stood their ground despite Nebuchadnezzar's threat and action. If you say you were in minority even as a captive, and so could not disobey the law that compelled everybody to worship nobody else but the king, He will call Daniel to come and tell you his story.

If you say you renounced your faith in the Lord because of the so many imprisonments and tortures you went through, He will readily call Paul to testify of what he went through. We can go on and on.

That is why scripture says that we are inexcusable.

All these people and many more had eternity in focus. And it influenced their attitudes and actions, or decisions. They understood that eternity is the place of permanent abode, not here on earth. That whereas we could live for up to 120 years (rarely) here on earth, we will live for uncountable years, that is, eternally in eternity. So indeed, we are just pilgrims here.

We must note that eternity can only be spent in one place. If we meet God's standard of holiness and purity till the end, then we will spend eternity with our God and the saints. Otherwise, we spend eternity in hell with Satan and his demons where there will be weeping and gnashing of teeth. May that never be our portion in Jesus name, Amen!

If we then hope to share eternity with our Lord and Savior Jesus Christ, then we must walk in integrity here on earth. We must purify ourselves, 1 John 3:1-3 says *"Behold, what manner of love the Father had bestowed upon us, that we should be called the sons of God, therefore the world knoweth us not, because it knew him not. Beloved, now are we the sons of God, and it doth not yet appear what we shall be, but we know that, when He shall appear, we shall be like Him; for we shall see Him as He is. And every man that hath this hope in him purifieth himself even as He is pure"*.

Note: verse three carefully. It says that we must purify ourselves: to walk and live with integrity is an integral part of purification. And one of the primary reasons for living a life of integrity is to share eternity with our God.

FEED ON THE WORD

Jeremiah. 15:16 says *"Thy words were found, and I did eat them, and they word was unto me the joy and rejoicing of mine heart, for I am called by thy name, O Lord God of hosts"*. So we can indeed feed on the word of God the same way we feed with our physical food. As our physical or natural food nourishes us physically, so does the word of God nourish us spiritually. As our physical body digests and then assimilates the physical food, to give the needed nourishment to our physical body, so also does the word of God have the ability to permeate our spiritual body to produce the desired spiritual nourishment. See what Heb. 4:12 says: *"For the word of God is quick and powerful, and sharper than any two-edged sword, piercing even to the dividing asunder of soul and spirit and of the joints and marrow, and is a discerner of the thoughts and intents of the heart".*

The word of God has the ability to sharpen and shape up every one of us to a better modus vivendi, modus operandi and modus preparandi. It is powerful enough to change the course of our lives for the better even in a short while, it says it is "quick and powerful". It can bulldoze any obstacles in its way, that is why it is so sharp and even has a piercing ability, that is, forcefully penetrating difficult and stubborn areas of our lives, whether it is stubbornness or habits that have refused to leave us, like besetting sins. It can cast down imaginations and everything that exalts itself against the knowledge of God. Look, also, at what it says in Ps. 119:105 *"Thy word is a lamp unto my feet, and a light unto my path"*. So, the word of God has the ability to guide you in the parts of righteousness, in the parts of integrity, and in the parts of holiness. It makes sure that you do not walk in the counsel of the ungodly, nor stand in the way of sinners, nor sit in the seat of the scornful (Ps. 1:1). The scripture says that any man that does not do these things is blessed. Why? Because definitely your delight then is in the law (will) of the Lord, because you strive to keep or obey it. You are then likened to a tree planted by the rivers of water that brings forth his fruit in his season; his leaf does not wither and whatever he does prospers (see Ps. 1:1-3). So we continuously meditate on the word of God, and apply it to our everyday activities, it brings us both material, physical and spiritual prosperity. No wonder Josh. 1:8 says, *"this book of the law (the word of God) shall not depart out of thy mouth: but thou shalt meditate therein day and night, that thou mayest observe to do according to all that is written therein: for then thou shalt make thy way prosperous, and then thou shall have good success".*

That reminds me of the story that was told about an oil prospecting company that went to Israel to search for oil. After making several efforts in different locations in Israel without success, one of the workers of the company who knew the scriptures remembered Deut. 33:24 where the Bible said; *"and of Asher he said, let Asher be blessed with children: let him be acceptable to his brethren, and LET HIM DIP HIS FOOT IN OIL"* (emphasis mine). Jacob, said this when he was about to die as he started giving fatherly blessing to all his twelve children that made up the twelve tribes of Israel. Asher was one of those children and by extension, a tribe that had a geographical location in Israel. So this company staff told his colleagues that they should actually find out the geographical location of Asher in Israel and prospect for oil there. And when they did, they found oil. I had also listened to Pastor Enoch. A Adeboye, the General Overseer of Redeemed Christian Church of God (RCCG) give the testing of how he had a difficulty for many weeks in solving a particular equation while he was writing his thesis during his Ph.D program in Mathematics. Hear him: "When I was writing my Ph.D thesis, I got to a point where I had one hundred and eighty-six simultaneous equations and could not find a solution! One fateful day, I got tired of it all. I threw the project aside and picked up my Bible to do some studying. I read the passage where God parted the Red Sea for the Israelites to cross (Exodus 14) and the Spirit of God spoke to me saying "that is the solution to your problem" I took the thesis again and this time around, I divided the equations into two categories, one on the left and the other on the right, just as the Red Sea parted to the left and to the right. I then solved both categories separately and got my final answer soon afterwards. The word of God set me on my feet academically. When I presented my thesis to the external examiner, he had no questions for me. He only said to the authorities, Give this young man his Ph.D". That is the power in the word of God for you.

The Psalmist in Ps. 119:9, asks a question and also answers it. He asks *"where withal shall a young man cleans his way? By taking heed thereto according to thy word"* (KJV). See how the NLT puts it: *"How can a young man stay pure? By obeying your word"*. So purity comes by obedience to the word of God. And I had earlier stated that integrity is an integral part of purification. The word of God can come to you in many ways. It can come as a rhema (revealed word) while you are studying the Bible like in the stories of the oil prospecting company in Israel and the case of Pastor E. A. Adeboye. They were studying the word when the revelations came to them. And it prospered them. That is why Joshua 1:8 says *"This book of the law (word of God) shall not depart out of thy mouth; but thou shalt meditate therein day and night, that thou mayest observe to do according to all that is written therein: for then thou shalt make thy way prosperous, and then thou shalt have good success"*. Feeding on the word of God prospers us both spiritually and physically, (materially, financial, maritally, academically, etc).

It gives you good success, not a bad success that is like a phyrric victory.

Spiritually it enhances your understanding of the person, personality and purposes of God. It instills the fear of God in you which makes you pursue that which is right, and run away from that which is wrong and evil. Your knowledge of the word of God stops you from being *"tossed to and fro, and carried about with every wind of doctrine, by the sleight of men, and cunning craftiness, whereby they lie in wait to deceive"* as Paul wrote in Eph. 4:14. And that way you will neither be ashamed or be brought to shame.

2 Tim. 2:15 says *"Study to show thyself approved unto God, a workman that needeth not be ashamed, rightly dividing the word of truth"*. You can only divide (interpret and implement) the word of God rightly when you study it and medicate on it regularly. As I have said earlier, it is a sure way of being delivered from shame. There is no alternative to it. You must obey the word of God.

The other way we can receive the word of God is when God Himself or by His spirit speaks to us.

Remember, for example, when the children of Israel left Egypt to go to the Promised Land being led by Moses, the servant of the Lord. A time came when they got to the Red Sea, and there was no way to pass. Remember that at this time, Pharaoh and the Egyptians where in hot pursuit of the Israelites. So they became panicky because they were now between the Red Sea and Pharaoh and the Egyptian. They began to cry. But God spoke His word to Moses and said in Ex. 14:15-16 *"And the Lord said unto Moses, wherefore criest thou unto me? Speak unto the children of Israel that they go forward: but lift thou up thy rod, and stretch out thine hand over the sea, and divide it; and the children of Israel shall go on dry ground through the midst of the sea"*. Moses did exactly according to the WORD OF GOD. And of course, the Israelites crossed the Red Sea as on dry ground, just because Moses obeyed the word of God.

We must come to the realization of the power in the word of God. He created the whole universe by merely speaking the word. There is creative power in the word. During creation, God said in Gen. 1:3 *"Let there be light, and there was light"* In v6, *"and God said, let there be a firmament in the midst of the waters, and let it divide the waters from the waters"*. Just opening His mouth to speak, and the whole world came into existence. No wonder the gospel according to Apostle John. 1:1 says *"In the beginning was the word, and the word was with God, and the word was God"*. So we can now understand why the word of God is very potent. Because the word is God Himself epitomized. With all that has so far been enunciated about the word of God and the power it carries, there is therefore no way you could be "word-full" and not be wonderful in your relationship with God. That is, there is no way you can make the word of God an integral part of your life, and not walk with integrity.

09

THE BLESSINGS OF INTEGRITY

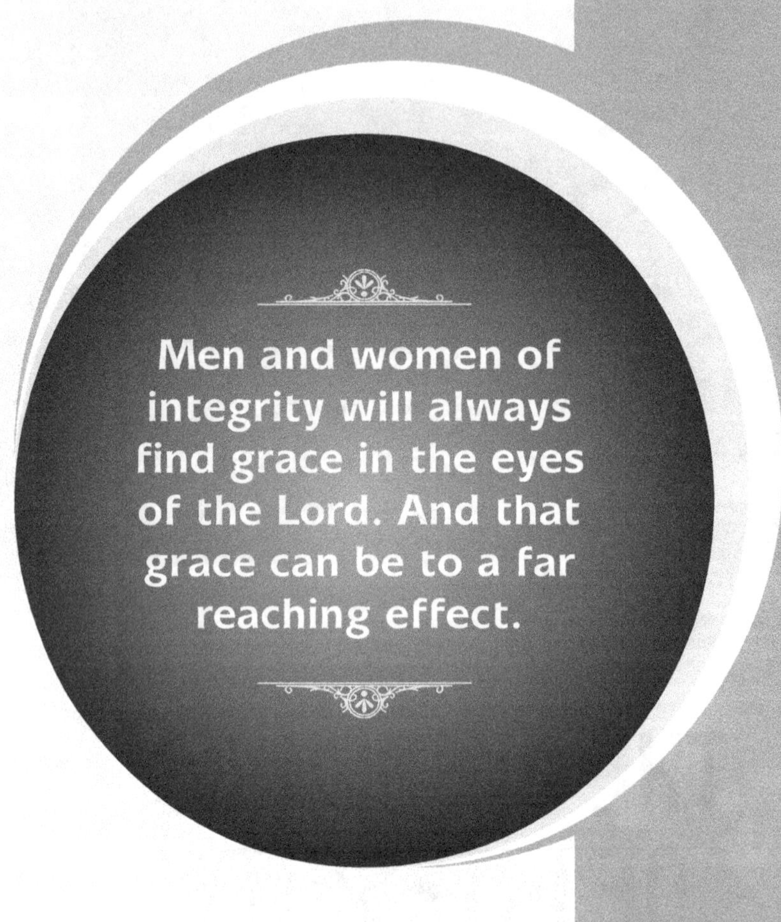
Men and women of integrity will always find grace in the eyes of the Lord. And that grace can be to a far reaching effect.

Nine

CHAPTER NINE

THE BLESSINGS OF INTEGRITY

Isa. 33:15-16 (NLT)

> *"Those who are honest and fair, who refuse to profit by fraud, who stay far away from bribes, who refuse to listen to those who plot murder, who shut their eyes to all enticement to do wrong – these are the ones who will dwell on high. The rocks of the mountains will be their fortress. Food will be supplied to them, and they will have water in abundance".*

The story of Noah in Genesis chapter 7 is a classic example of the reward for integrity. When terrible iniquity abounded in all the earth in the days of Noah, that virtually every man and woman out there were entrenched in evil doings, there was still a man out there who epitomized integrity. In Gen. 7:1 *"The Lord said unto Noah, come thou and all thy house into the ark; for thee have I seen righteous before me in this generation"*. What a testimony God Himself gave concerning a man! For God indeed had decided to destroy everything He had created.

Scripture says in Gen. 6:6-7; *"And it repented the Lord that he made man on the earth, and it grieved him at his heart". (7) "And the Lord said, I will destroy man whom I have created from the face of the earth, both man and beast, and the creeping thing, and the fowls of the air; for it repenteth me that I have made them".*

Verse 8 says "*But Noah found grace in the eyes of the Lord".*

Men and women of integrity will always find grace in the eyes of the Lord. And that grace can be to a far reaching effect.

Imagine that the only people on earth God decided to spare was Noah and his family! Which blessing of integrity could be better than this?

Remember that the Bible says that "*The righteous shall inherit the land, and dwell therein forever (Ps: 37:29).*

Righteousness (integrity) will always exalt (Ps. 14:34), it will always make the difference between the exalted and debased. Nothing exalts one to the topmost position and keeps you there like integrity. Integrity brings dignity and honour. It also has a preservative as well as protective ability which eventually enhances longevity.

Another biblical character that benefitted immensely from his integrity was Joseph. After he was sold into slavery by his brothers to the Ishmaelite, he was brought into Egypt and an officer of Pharaoh, Potiphar, bought him. Potiphar brought Joseph to his house, and when he noticed that the Lord was with Joseph, and that whatever he did prospered. (Gen. 39:3-4), he made Joseph overseer over his house, and all that he had, he put into Joseph's hand.

The Bible records in Gen. 39:7 that *"It came to pass after these things,that his master's wife cast her eyes upon Joseph, and she said (to him), lie with me".*

Joseph's response to this terrible temptation which many of us would have fallen prey to was what marked him out clearly as a man of integrity. He said in response (V8) *"But he refused and said unto his master's wife, behold, my master wotheth not what is with me in the house, and he hath committee all that he hath to my hand". V9 "There is none greater in this house than I, neither hath he kept back anythingfrom me but thee, because thou art his wife: How can I do this great wickedness, and sin against God?*

Though this stand of Joseph eventually and wrongfully landed him in prison, but that imprisonment was the eventual stepping stone prepared by God to promote him to the number two citizen in Egypt. So it is pertinent to know that your stand for integrity can bring you some hardship initially, but that is temporary. Remember that when Micaiah the prophet told Ahab King of Israel what will be his true fate if he went to battle at Ramothglead against the king of Syria, he became angry and commanded that Micaiah be sent to prison and be fed with the bread of affliction. But eventually God vindicated Micaiah.

Scripture says in 1 Cor. 4:17 *"For our light affliction which is but for a moment, worketh for us a far more exceeding and eternal weight of glory".*

The plot against you as a man of integrity could be the plan of God to promote you. That was exactly what happened to

Joseph, because if he was not sent to prison, he would not possibly have met with Pharoah's baker and butler who he interpreted their dreams accurately. It was that dream interpretation that eventually brought him to Pharoah who also had two similar dreams which his magicians and wise men could not interpret. It was then that the chief butler remembered Joseph who interpreted his dream. By then two good years had passed and Joseph was still in prison. (Gen. 10:11-23, 41:1-45).

Joseph not only interpreted the dreams of Pharoah, but he also gave counsel of what should be done in Egypt to avert severe famine. Suddenly by divine intervention, Joseph was promoted from prisoner to prime minister, the second most important person in Egypt. That was the blessing of integrity.

There are many other people in the Bible who exhibited utmost integrity. Even Abraham, the father of faith exhibited both integrity and selflessness. When God called him to leave his country, and his kindred and go to a place He (God) would show him (Gen. 12) He took Lot, his brother's son along with him. Both Abraham and Lot, each had a great number of herds and flocks and tents, but at a point in time, the land was no longer able to contain both of them. And strife developed between the herdsmen of Abraham and those of Lot. Abraham, a selfless man of integrity told Lot that they didn't have to quarrel over land or grazing fields. He told him that since there was land enough around them; hear Abraham, *"And Abram said unto Lot, let there be no strife, I pray thee, between me and thee, and between my herdsmen and thy herdsmen; for we be brethren. Is not the whole land before thee? Separate thyself, I pray thee from me: if thou wilt take the left land, then I will go to the right; or if thou depart to the right hand, then I will go to the left. And Lot lifted up his eyes, and beheld all the plain of Jordan, that is well watered everywhere, before the Lord destroyed Sodom and Gomorrah, even as the garden of the Lord, like the land of Egypt, as thou comest unto Zoar. Then Lot chose him all the plain of Jordan, and Lot journeyed east: and they separated themselves one from the other"* (Gen. 14).

Remember that one of the definitions of integrity is "Possession of firm Godly principles".

Abraham, who should have chosen the part of the land he wanted because after-all he was much older, and even brought Lot to the place, decided to allow Lot to choose first, all in order to avoid strife!! Only a man of integrity can do that.

Furthermore when Lot was taken captive together with his family and goods, Abraham and his army of 318 men that he trained in his house went to war and rescued Lot and family (Gen. 14:1-12).

You may be tempted to ask; where is the blessing of integrity here. See what the Bible says in Gen. 15:4-5) *"After these things, the word of Lord came unto Abram in a vision, saying, fear not, Abram: I am thy shield and thy exceeding great reward. And Abram said, Lord God, what wilt thou give me, seeing I go childless, and the steward in my house is this Eliezer of Damascus?...and behold, the word of the Lord came unto him, saying , this will not be thine heir; but he that shall come forth out of thine own bowels shall be thine heir. And he brought him forth abroad, and said, look now toward heaven, and tell the stars, if thou be able to number them; and he said unto him, so shall thy seed be".* So Abram was rewarded with a promise of fruitfulness and to be the father of the nations, which was eventually fulfilled in the birth of Isaac. Today, we are the seeds of Abraham. And beside the blessings of fruitfulness, he was also blessed with the inheritance of land (V7).

Let us consider Ruth, the daughter in-law of Noami. After the death of her husband and father in-law when they were sojourning in Moab, her mother in-law, Naomi, decided to leave Moab to return to Judah. Noami's two daughters in-law decided that they would follow her to return to Judah, but Noami insisted that they should go back to their people and possibly get married again and live a better life since she had no male child again to give them as husbands. Orpah, one of her daughter's in-law agreed and returned to her people. But Ruth insisted that she would follow Noami back to Judah. Hear her (Ruth 1:16-17) *"Intreat me not to leave thee, or to return from following after thee; for whither thou goest, I will go; and where thou lodgest, I will lodge; thy people shall be my people and thy God, my God. Where thou diest, will I die, and there will I be buried; the Lord do so to me, and more also, if ought but death part thee and me".*

This was a classical show of possession of firm principles which is one of our definitions of integrity.

And we saw that at the end of it all, Ruth eventually, married Boaz, a kinsman of Elimelech, Naomi's late husband. Boaz and Ruth had a son who was named Obed.

Obed eventually was the father of Jesse, the father of David (Ruth 4:17-21). Our Lord and Saviour Jesus Christ is genealogically traced to the lineage of David (See Matt. 1:17). Today, you cannot exhaustively trace the earthly genealogy of Jesus Christ without mentioning Ruth. What can be more glorious and rewarding!! That was as a result of her resoluteness!.

What of Mordecai, the step-father of Queen Esther. In Esther 2:21-23, story has it that, two of king's Ahasuerus eunuchs who guarded the door at the king's private quarters became angry with him and plotted to assassinate the king. But Mordecai who was on duty at the King's gate heard about it, and gave the information to Queen Esther who then told the king about it and gave Mordecai credit for the report. The king's life was eventually spared. And this act of integrity was recorded in the Book of History of the king. The whole matter was apparently forgotten. But on this particular night, a night in which coincidentally Haman had prepared a gallow to execute Mordecai, the king was troubled. He could not sleep, and he ordered an attendant to bring the book of history of his reign, so it could be read to him (Esther 6:1-12). In the book he discovered on account of how Mordecai had exposed the plot of Bigthane and Teres, who planned to assassinate the king. On further inquiry, he discovered that no reward had been given to Mordecai for this. Then he ordered Haman that was planning to execute Mordecai to honor him (Mordecai) in a new robe and on the horse the king himself had ridden – one with a royal emblem on its head. Mordecai, the gateman, became an instant celebrity for his integrity. God is both a recorder and a rewarder.

In Act 10:1, the BIBLE tells us about a Roman army officer (Centurion) who was describe as *" a devout man, and one that feared God with all his house, which gave much alms to the people, and prayed to God always."*

This is nothing else but the description that could only be given to a man of integrity. The blessings of integrity are not only physical or material. They could also be spiritual which are indeed of greater eternal relevance. The blessing Cornelius received for his integrity was spiritual. It was on record that before Cornelius and his family experienced the Baptism of Holy Ghost, no other Gentile, individual or family had had that experience. Scripture said in Act. 10:44 That *"while Peter yet spake these words the Holy Ghost fell on all them which heard the word"*. Even Peter and those who came with him were astonished about this experience of the Gentile. Vs46 said *"For they heard them speak with tongues and magnify God"*. Except you have had this same experience of baptism of the Holy Ghost, you may not understand what an exciting experience it would have been to Cornelius and his family. It is an unquantifiable blessing indeed. Their lives never remained the same from that very day.

The Bible is filled with many stories of men and women who were blessed extraordinarily because of different levels or forms of integrity they exhibited. A good example is Mary the Mother of Jesus. She was tremendously blessed among other Virgins to become the earthly mother of our Lord and savior Jesus Christ. You can agree with me that Mary was not just any other virgin in the streets of Galilee or Israel, who though had kept her virginity but was involved in other vices or character threats. The way Angel

Gabriel greeted her even spoke volumes. See Lk. 1:28 *"And the Angel came in unto her and said, Hail, thou that art highly favoured, the Lord is with thee. Blessed art thou among women".* The above greeting from the angel "thou that art highly favoured, the Lord is with thee" speaks volumes on the reputation and integrity of Mary. Saying that *"blessed art thou among women" meant that she was a peculiar women, different and special with great qualities other women in her time did not possess".*

Obviously, there must have been other virgins in the days of Mary. So we see that integrity as it were has a very wide scope of definition, not a parochial one.

INTEGRITY AND BOLDNESS

One of the benefit of integrity is the boldness it gives. The Bible says in Prov, 28:1 that *"The righteous are bold as a lion".* A man of integrity does not usually have any "skeletons" in his cupboard. That is, he has nothing to hide and he is not afraid of any criticism that may be brought against him in the public domain because he is sure of all his actions and can always satisfactorily explain whatever action he has taken on any issue. He will always be bold to ask you to go and verify. And the criticism will eventually turn out to be spurious and unfounded. Consider Peter Obi, the presidential candidate of the Labour Party in the 2023 general elections in Nigeria, and indeed the winner of that election. He has an impeccable record of integrity and despite every attempt of his opponents to bring spurious accusations, none was able to sale. It was his integrity that turned the "OBI-DIENT MOVEMENT" into a tsunami that swept away many politicians and retired them permanently! That is contrary to the attitude of the wicked or the unrighteous. Scripture says *"The wicked flee when no man pursueth"* (Prov. 28:1). Can you imagine that "even when nobody is pursuing him, he is running away, why? Because he has full realization of the atrocities he has committed against either individual business associates, communities or corporate bodies. He knows that some of these people are bitter and will seize any opportunity at their disposal to avenge for themselves. So the wicked keeps hiding and running from his perceived enemies, even when they've not started coming after him. That is the genesis of what we now see rampant in our society. So many young men and women now going around with escorts of either policemen, soldiers or even their own privately engaged security. This is not to say that everyone that goes around with security escorts is a wicked man. However, all we are saying is that the guilty are afraid. That is why the more crime increases in our society, the more people you see moving around with security escorts. Some of those who have those escorts are neck deep in the commission of those crimes, whether in governance or out of it. They have lost their boldness, but are now applying artificial boldness. If you for example read 1 Sam.12:1-5, you will notice how Samuel who judged Israel for many years boldly asserted his integrity before the people. It reads: *"And Samuel said unto all Israel, behold I have hearkened unto your voice in all that ye said unto me, and have made a king over you. And now, behold, the king walketh before you: and I am old and gray headed; and behold my sons are with you; and I have walked before you from my childhood unto this day. Behold, here I am: witness against me before the lord, and before his anointed: whose Ox have I taken? Or whose ass have I taken? Or of whose hand have I received any bribe to blind mine eyes therewith? And I will restore it for you. And they said, Thou hast not defrauded us, nor oppressed us, ought thou taken neither of any man's hand. And he said unto them, the Lord is witness against you, and his anointed is witness this day, that ye have not found ought in my hand. And they answered, He is witness"*

This is simply incredible! What a testimony. How many persons in position of leadership today can have the temerity or audacity to ask the people they're leading the above question? I mean both political and spiritual leadership. Today almost every leader falls as a result of one banana peel or the other. But for Samuel, he stood like the rock of Gibraltar no matter what happened. No wonder he was able to rebuke and remove King Saul when he disobeyed without looking back. He had the boldness to do it because even though he anointed Saul king, he never came to him to ask for any gratifications of any type. So his integrity was intact.

That is why the Bible says in 2 Cor.10:6 (NLT): "*And after you have become fully obedient*". That is to say, you cannot have a log in your eyes and without removing it you go to remove a small speck in somebody else eye. That is nothing but hypocrisy. One can only handle disobedience when he is completely obedient in the first place. This is what has killed the anointing in today's church. But this is very common place in the political arena, where the makers of the law are the number one breakers of the law.

If it was today, what Saul would have done would be to send some of the fattened calves he brought from Amalek (Contrary to the instructions of the Lord) to Samuel and he would look the other way when the instruction of the Lord that came out through his own mouth were being flagrantly disobeyed by Saul and his army.

The practice of settlement has so badly eroded whatever is left of our integrity. It has permeated every fabric of both our public and even ecclesiastical institution today. In many of our main churches, even the Pentecostal, ministers even "Settle" their superiors to influence their postings to particular churches or towns of their choice. If this is happening in the church of Jesus Christ amongst ministers of the gospel themselves, you could imagine what the situation is with the secular world like in our government ministries and parastatals. It is just the order of the day.

In the same vein, this same settlement of a thing is the reason why contracts are most inflated in Nigeria, even to the tone of more than one thousand percent (1000%). It is the reason why there are uncompleted gigantic and white elephant projects littered all over the country. It is the reason why round pegs are put in square holes in terms of appointments. We can go on and on. All you need is to settle the awarders of the contract as well as the superiors. They will look the other way and allow you to have your way. Even when you don't eventually finish the contract, it doesn't matter. After all they have been settled upfront.

This same issue of settle has even overtaken our

educational system and eroded it. It is called "sorting" in the tertiary institutions. Your ability to sort out the lecturers will determine the grades you will get in your courses and even the class of degree you will have. That is why today some people will come out with first class or second class upper degrees, yet they know nothing. I did not say it is always the case. But it is happening. Today a professor can write the masters or Ph.D thesis of his student at a fee (settlement). Many Masters and doctorate degree holders today are like "Chinese or Taiwan" products of those days, meaning they are of very substandard qualities. But the tragedy is that these ones who have earned both their first and postgraduate degrees by "sorting", will eventually become the teachers and supervisors of the upcoming postgraduate students. You can therefore imagine what they will have to offer, or the quality of the products (Masters and doctorate graduates) they will produce. This is why the quality of education in our country has continued to nose-dive.

Finally on the benefits of integrity, Heb. 1:9 says *"thou hast loved righteousness, and hated iniquity; therefore God, even they God, had anointed thee with the oil of gladness above thy fellows"*.

Another benefit of integrity is anointing from God. Anointing is like an investiture with divine or heavenly prowess. This investiture is with an overflow of gladness beyond the ordinary. It's like having a continuous merry heart. Remember, Prov. 17:22 says *"A mercy heart doeth good like medicine..."*

Also Prov. 15:15b says *"he that is of a merry heart hath a continual feast"*. And this kind of person is living a blissful life without stress. This obviously brings longevity as one of its benefits. So living a life of righteousness or integrity is a highway to longevity.

www.ingramcontent.com/pod-product-compliance
Lightning Source LLC
LaVergne TN
LVHW050543160826
845677LV00011B/2155